COMBAT LEGEND

SR-71
BLACKBIRD

Paul F. Crickmore

Airlife

In Memory of Mum.

Acknowledgements

My sincere thanks go to the many friends who have served in the Senior Crown programme and who have been so patient, kind and helpful over the years. In particular I would like to single out Don Emmons, Rich Graham, Tim Brown, Kent Burns, Denny Lombard, Jay Murphy, Jay Miller, Chris Pocock and Jeff Richelson.

Thanks also to my Editor and friend Paul E. Eden

Last but by no means least, I'd like to thank my wife Ali, for her love, help and support in all my endeavours and Nic, for all the fun she has brought with her

Information on plastic model kits supplied by H. G. Hannant Ltd: www.hannants.co.uk

Copyright © 2002 Airlife Publishing Ltd

Text written by Paul F. Crickmore
Colour profiles created by Dave Windle

First published in the UK in 2002
by Airlife Publishing Ltd

British Library Cataloguing-in-Publication Data
A catalogue record for this book
is available from the British Library

ISBN 1 84037 382 2

Printed in Hong Kong

For a complete list of all Airlife titles please contact:

Airlife Publishing Ltd
101 Longden Road, Shrewsbury, SY3 9EB, England
E-mail: sales@airlifebooks.com
Website: www.airlifebooks.com

Contents

1. Prototypes and Development: the A-12 Story

When, as Sir Winston Churchill put it, 'an "Iron Curtain" descended across the Continent', following the end of the Second World War, and relations between the victorious eastern and western powers chilled into the so-called Cold War, it was soon realised by the Allies that maps of the Soviet Union and the Warsaw Pact countries, necessary for target-planning the unthinkable, were completely inadequate. Another thing missing was the West's ability to compile accurate and detailed intelligence estimates regarding the industrial, military and technical capabilities of communist states. Human intelligence sources (Humint), or spies, were only partially successful in plugging some of these gaps, largely due to the closed nature of communist society and the ruthless efficiency of the KGB (state security police) and GRU.

Given the vastness of the USSR and the state of prevailing technology at the time, the only realistic answer to the problem was manned reconnaissance overflight. But the wanton violation of a sovereign state's airspace is contrary to international law. Should therefore such operations go ahead, they would need to be

In the SR-71, the US had an invaluable reconnaissance asset that had proved invulnerable to interception over three decades of Mach-3+ operations. The dire effects of its premature retirement were still being felt as the US led international operations against the Al-Qaeda terrorist organisation in Afghanistan in 2001-02. On 6 October 1981, '964, callsign MINTY 23, participated in a Barents/Baltic Sea sortie. (Paul F. Crickmore)

conducted under conditions of great secrecy, gaining prior approval from the US President and or the British Prime Minister or other NATO leaders; for approval to be granted, such planned incursions would also need to stand a good chance of success. Initially such hazardous missions were flown by extremely brave flight crews in converted bombers. However, as Soviet anti-aircraft technology continued to develop, it became increasingly apparent that a purpose-built aircraft, capable of operating at extreme altitude was required in order to provide the prerequisite margin of success. The result was a programme operated by the Central Intelligence Agency (CIA), codenamed Project Aquatone. The aircraft, designed by aeronautical engineering genius, Clarence L. 'Kelly' Johnson, was the Lockheed U-2. Kelly and his team worked in an area secure from the rest of the Lockheed Burbank plant that came to be known as the 'Skunk Works', a name derived from a cartoon strip.

The first U-2 overflight of the Soviet Union, designated Mission 2013, was conducted by Agency pilot Hervey Stockman, on 4 July 1956; during that 8 hour 45 minute flight, the aircraft's A-2 camera system acquired outstanding imagery of known bomber bases near Minsk, the naval shipyards at Leningrad and yet more bomber bases in the Baltic States, before recovering safely back at Wiesbaden Air Base, West Germany. Four further U-2 overflights were conducted in rapid succession, on 5, 9 and 10 July (two missions were flown on 9 July). But the 10 July mission also brought with it the first

of many Soviet protest notes objecting to the 'violation of the air frontiers of the Soviet Union by American aircraft [that] cannot be interpreted as other than intentional and conducted for the purposes of reconnaissance'. As a result, President Eisenhower ordered the CIA to call an immediate halt to such operations until further notice. However, once the invaluable photographic imagery had been processed and analysed, a CIA memo dated 17 July noted that 'there can be no doubt of the value in terms of our national security of the photographic coverage obtained on 4 July 1956 of five of the seven highest priority targets specified by the

Driving the A-12 programme was the need to develop a reconnaissance platform more survivable than the high-flying, but slow, U-2. Aircraft 56-6701, U-2B Article 368, was delivered to Groom Lake in March 1957. It was later assigned to the Special Projects Branch at the US Air Force Flight Test Centre, Edwards AFB, California. (Lockheed)

USAF'. It continued 'for the first time we are really able to say that we have an understanding of much of what was going on', and concluded that to bar further overflights would be tragic, as it would lead to guesswork being used when drawing up policies pertaining to the USSR, and asserted that such policies could well endanger US foreign relations to a far greater extent than continuing the overflight programme.

The overflights were resumed in late November, but they remained sporadic, due to Eisenhower's concern about a possible Soviet reaction. Such misgivings were not the sole preserve of the President; Aquatone's CIA programme manager, Richard Bissell Jr, and even Kelly Johnson, were under no illusions about the U-2's possible vulnerability; all they hoped for was a couple of good years, as the Soviets' ability to detect and track the frail-

Several studies for a U-2 replacement were conducted by Kelly Johnson and his team of Skunk Works engineers. Arrow I is shown above, while Archangel I (below) dated from October 1957. Archangel II (left), was second in the design evolution and was to be powered by two turbojets inboard and two ramjets outboard. (all Lockheed Martin Skunk Works)

looking subsonic aircraft from the beginning had come as a great shock to both the Agency and Lockheed.

In August 1957, the Scientific Engineering Institute (SEI), a Boston-based CIA proprietary already working on ways of reducing the U-2's vulnerability, began studies to investigate the possibilities of designing an aircraft with a small radar cross-section (RCS). The SEI soon discovered that flight at supersonic speed and high altitude, when combined with a reduced RCS, dramatically reduced the chances of radar detection. These findings then became the CIA's criteria for a successor to the U-2 and were passed on to both Lockheed and the Convair Division of General Dynamics as a basis for further research on the understanding that initial design submissions would be non-funded and non-contracted.

Both companies accepted the challenge and were assured that funding would be forthcoming at the appropriate time. For the next 12 months, the Agency received designs that were both developed and refined, all at no expense! It was apparent to Bissell that the cost of developing such an advanced aircraft would be both high risk and extremely expensive; government funding would be a prerequisite and to obtain this, various high-ranking government officials would have to be cleared into the programme and given clear, authoritative presentations on advances as they occurred. Therefore to assist in the evaluation process, Bissell turned to Edwin Land to serve as chairman of an advisory group.

Technical Capabilities Panel

Land had previously served on Project Three of the Technical Capabilities Panel (TCP) that had proved to be staunch supporters of the U-2 design. Other members of the new panel included Edward Purcell – another former TCP member, Allan Donovan of the Cornell Aeronautical Laboratory and Bissell's assistant Eugene Kiefer. The group met on some six occasions, usually in Land's Cambridge, Massachusetts, office, together with representatives from the Air Force, Navy and senior design engineers from the two competing aircraft companies. In September 1957, the panel rejected two hydrogen-powered designs; one, a

The second A-12 to be built was mounted on a pole and used during RCS tests. A similar technique was used years later with the F-117 'Stealth Fighter'. (Lockheed Martin Skunk Works)

Navy-Boeing proposal for a 190-ft (56-m) long inflatable aircraft, the other from Lockheed, codenamed Suntan. Two later submissions from the Skunk Works were also rejected – a tailless, subsonic aircraft with a very small RCS and a supersonic design, designated A-2. The group approved further work on a Convair design, codenamed Fish; this Mach 4, ramjet-powered vehicle was, it was planned, to be air-launched from a Convair B-58 Hustler.

During a late November 1958 meeting, the panel again reviewed the Fish programme together with Lockheed's newest proposal, the A-3, and concluded from the submissions that the initial concept of a high-Mach, high-altitude, low-RCS vehicle remained robust. Eisenhower had been kept up-to-date on the projects' progress by Dr James Killian, the first presidential scientific advisor; and following a briefing on 17 December from the CIA's Director of Intelligence (DCI), Allen Dulles, Bissell, Land and Purcell approved funds for further research for the programme, which was now designated Project Gusto.

During a July 1959 meeting, the advisory board again rejected both companies' submissions, the Fish proposal on the basis that its ramjet engines were unproven and therefore high risk; and the

Lockheed A-11 proposal due to its large RCS. Lockheed had already seen its proposals A-4 to A-10 come to nothing. On 20 August 1959, final submissions from both companies were made to a joint DoD/Air Force/CIA selection panel. Lockheed's A-12 and Convair's Kingfish designs, although strikingly different in appearance, proposed a similar performance envelope:

Project	A-12	Kingfish
Speed	Mach 3.2	Mach 3.2
Range (total)	4,120 nm	4,000 nm
	(7634 km)	(7412 km)
Range (at	3,800 nm	3,400 nm
altitude)	(7041 km)	(6300 km)
Cruise altitudes:		
Start	84,500 ft	85,000 ft
	(25756 m)	(25908 m)
Mid-range	91,000 ft	88,000 ft
	(27737 m)	(26822 m)
End	97,600 ft	94,000 ft
	(29748 m)	(28651 m)
Length	102 ft (31.09 m)	79 ft 6 in
		(24.23 m)
Span	57 ft (17.37 m)	56 ft (17.07 m)
Gross weight	110,000 lb	101,700 lb
	(49895 kg)	(46130 kg)
Fuel Weight	64,600 lb	62,000 lb
	(29302 kg)	(28123 kg)
First Flight	22 months	22 months

On 28 August 1959, Kelly was informed by John Parangosky – Gusto's CIA programme director, that the Skunk Works was provisional winner of the competition, provided that it was able to considerably reduce the aircraft's RCS by 1 January 1960. The next day the Lockheed company was given the official go-ahead, with initial funding of $4.5 million approved to cover the period 1 September to 1 January 1960. Project Gusto was now at an end and a new codename, Oxcart, was assigned.

Oxcart authorisation

On 3 September, the Agency authorised Lockheed to proceed with anti-radar studies, aerodynamic and structural tests, together with engineering designs. The small engineering team, under the supervision of Ed Martin, consisted of Dan Zuck in charge of cockpit design, Dave Robertson fuel system requirements, Henry Combs and Dick Bochme structures, as well as Dick Fuller, Burt McMaster and Kelly's protege Ben Rich. The studies resulted in a contract being signed on 1 February 1960, calling for Lockheed to produce twelve A-12 aircraft, at a cost of $96.6 million.

On 1 May 1960, just four months later, the decision to proceed with the A-12 must have seemed fully vindicated, following the shoot-down, by a barrage of SA-2 surface-to-air

The A-12s were known to their CIA pilots by the name Cygnus – after the star formation believed to harbour a black hole. Here one of the aircraft departs Area 51 after a test flight early in the programme. Note that the machine is unpainted. (Lockheed)

missiles (SAMs), of U-2 Article Number 360; and the subsequent capture of its Agency pilot, Francis Gary Powers, while on mission 4154 over Sverdlovsk, deep within the Soviet Union.

The ambitious performance sought in the new aircraft cannot be overstated; the best front line fighter aircraft of the day were the early century-series jets, like the F-100 Super Sabre and F-101 Voodoo. In a single bound, the A-12 would routinely operate at sustained speeds and altitudes treble and double respectively, of such contemporary fighters. The technical challenge facing the Skunk Works team was vast and the contracted time scale in which to achieve it was incredibly tight. Kelly would later remark that virtually everything on the aircraft had to be invented from scratch. When Lockheed's chief test pilot, Louis W. Schalk joined the team, work on refining the aircraft's design continued in parallel with additional construction work at the jet's secret test facility – Area 51 in Nevada.

The remote base, situated within the boundaries of the main Atomic Energy Commission (AEC) nuclear test site in Nevada, was first used for the U-2 programme; however, the site was in need of a major update and face-lift. A new water well was drilled and recreation facilities were provided for the construction workers, who were billeted in trailer houses. An 8,500-ft (2591-m) runway was constructed and 18 miles (5.5 km) of off-base highway was resurfaced to allow 500,000 US gal (1892650 litres) of special PF-1 fuel for the A-12 to be trucked in every month.

Three US Navy hangars together with Navy housing units were transported to the site in readiness for the arrival of the A-12 prototype, expected in May 1961. However, difficulties in procuring and working with titanium – the A-12's primary structural material, together with problems experienced by engine manufacturer Pratt & Whitney, soon began to compound and the anticipated first flight date slipped. Even when the completion date was put back to Christmas and the initial test flight postponed to late February 1962, the first J58s would still not be ready. Eventually Kelly decided that J75s would be used in the interim to propel the A-12 to a 'half-way house' of 50,000 ft (15240 m) and Mach 1.6, an action designed to take at least some of the pressure off the test team.

All the A-12s were constructed at Lockheed's Burbank Plant, then disassembled and moved by road to the Area 51 test site. (Lockheed Martin Skunk Works)

Crew selection

The flight crew selection process evolved by the Pentagon's Special Activities Office representative (Col Houser Wilson) and the Agency's USAF liaison officer (Brig. Gen. Jack Ledford, later succeeded by Brig. Paul Bacalis) got under way in 1961. On completion of the final screening, the first pilots were Kenneth Collins, Jack Layton, Francis Murray, Dennis Sullivan, Mele Vojvodich, Jack Weeks, William Skliar, Walter Ray, Alonzo Walter, David Young,

Every Cygnus pilot had his own personal callsign; here DUTCH 21, Ken Collins, is seen in his David Clark S-901 full pressure suit. The 'box' to his left is a portable oxygen and environmental control unit. (CIA)

and Russ Scott (although only the first six were destined to fly operational missions).

These elite pilots then began taking trips to the David Clark Company in Worcester, Massachusetts, to be outfitted with their own personal S-901 full pressure suits just like those worn by the Mercury and Gemini astronauts. In late 1961, Col Robert Holbury was appointed base commander of Area 51, his director of Flight Operations would be Col Doug Nelson and in the spring of 1962 eight F-101 Voodoos, to be used as companion trainers and pace/chase aircraft, plus two T-33s for pilot proficiency and a C-130 for cargo transportation, arrived at the remote base. A large 'restricted airspace zone' was enforced by the Federal Aviation Administration (FAA), to enhance security around 'the Area' and security measures were invoked upon North American Air Defense (NORAD) and FAA radar controllers, to ensure that fast-moving targets seen on their screens were not discussed. Planned air refuelling operations with Oxcart aircraft would be conducted by the 903rd Air Refuelling Squadron (ARS), which was located at Beale AFB, and equipped with Boeing KC-135Q Stratotanker tankers which possessed separate 'clean' tankage and plumbing to isolate the A-12's fuel from the tanker's standard JP-4. They also carried special ARC-50 distance-ranging radios for use in precision, long-distance, high-speed join-ups with the A-12s.

First flight

With the first A-12 now at last ready for final assembly, the entire fuselage, minus wings, was crated, covered with canvas and loaded on a special $100,000 trailer. At 2.30 a.m. on 26 February 1962, the slow-moving convoy left Burbank and arrived safely at Area 51 at 1.00 p.m., two days later. By 24 April, the airframe had been reassembled and engine test runs, together with low- and medium-speed taxi tests, had been successfully completed. It was now time for Lou Schalk to take the aircraft on a high-speed taxi run that would culminate in a momentary lift-off and landing roll-out onto the dry salty lake bed. For this first 'hop' the stability augmentation system (SAS) was left uncoupled; it would be properly tested in flight. As A-12, Article Number 121, accelerated down the runway, Lou recalled, "I had a very light load of fuel so it sort of accelerated really fast... I was probably three or four percent behind the aft limit centre of gravity when I lifted off the airplane... so it was unstable... immediately after lift-off, I really didn't think I was going to be able to put the airplane back on the ground safely because of lateral, directional and longitudinal oscillations. The airplane was very difficult to handle but I finally caught up with everything that was happening, got control back enough to set it back down, and chop engine power. Touchdown was on the lake bed instead of the runway, creating a tremendous cloud of dust into which I disappeared entirely. The tower controllers were calling me to find out what was happening and I was answering, but the UHF antenna was located on the underside of the airplane (for best transmission in flight) and no one could hear me. Finally, when I slowed down and started my turn on the lake bed and re-emerged from the dust cloud, everyone breathed a sigh of relief."

Two days later Lou took the Oxcart on a full flight. A faultless 7.05 a.m. take-off was followed shortly thereafter by all the left wing fillets being shed. Constructed from radar absorbent material (RAM), luckily these elements were non-structural and Lou recovered the aircraft back to Area 51 without further incident.

On 30 April, nearly a year behind schedule, Lou took the A-12 on its 'official' first flight. With appropriate government representatives on hand the 59 minute flight took the aircraft to a top speed of 340 kt (630 km/h) and altitude of 30,000 ft (9144 m). On 4 May, the aircraft went supersonic for the first time, reaching Mach 1.1. Kelly began to feel confident that the flight test programme would now progress rapidly, perhaps even recovering some of the time lost during the protracted manufacturing process. After Lou had completed the first thirteen flights, he was joined by Bill Park, another Lockheed test pilot. On 26 June, the second A-12 arrived at Area 51 and was immediately assigned to a three-month static RCS test programme. The third and fourth aircraft arrived during October and November; the latter was a two-seat A-12 trainer, nicknamed 'the Goose' by its crews, and was powered throughout its life by two J75s. On 5 October, another milestone was achieved when an A-12 flew for the first time with a J58, (a J75 was retained in the right nacelle until 15 January 1963, when the first fully J58-powered flight took place).

The U-2's vulnerability to SA-2 interception was again demonstrated in spectacular fashion during the Cuban Missile Crisis. During the course of a reconnaissance flight over the island on 27 October 1962, a salvo of missiles was fired

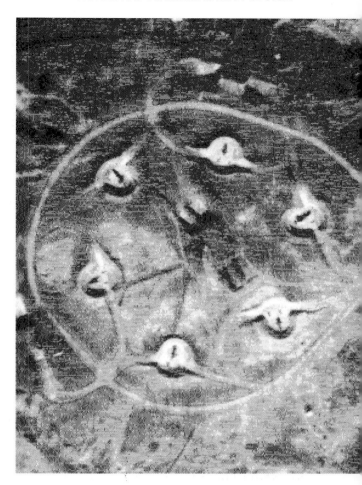

During a 26 January 1968 A-12 mission in search of the seized USS *Pueblo*, Frank Murray photographed most of North Korea, including this SA-2 site. (National Archive via Tim Brown)

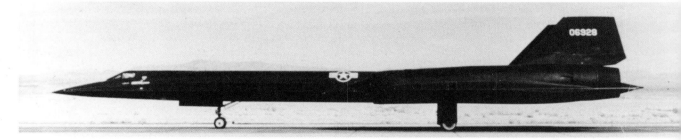

Later in their career A-12s sported an overall matt black paint scheme to help reduce airframe heat when cruising at high Mach. The scheme earned the A-12/SR-71 the popular 'Blackbird' name. The A-12 illustrated was lost during a test sortie on 5 January 1967; the pilot, Walt Ray, was killed. (CIA)

from the Banes naval base, located at the eastern end of the island. One of the SA-2 SAMs exploded above and behind U-2 Article 343, and jagged fragments of the exploding missile penetrated the cockpit and the pilot's pressure suit. Major Rudolph Anderson is presumed to have died as the cockpit depressurised and his suit failed to inflate.

Testing Soviet defences

As part of an effort to measure the range and power of various Soviet defence radar systems, the CIA implemented the Quality Elint (electronic intelligence) programme. A highly classified element of that programme was codenamed Palladium, and its objective was to determine the sensitivity of various Soviet radars. To achieve this, a special electronic transmitter, capable of projecting a 'ghost signal' had been developed. The knowledge gained from the Quality Elint power and coverage measurements enabled technicians to simulate an aircraft of any RCS and 'fly it' along any particular path at a predetermined speed and altitude. By electronically varying the size of the

radar returns and enlisting the co-operation of the National Security Agency (NSA), which intercepted and decrypted the relevant communications channels, it was possible to determine a radar's sensitivity based upon which signals were being tracked.

The construction of no less than nineteen SA-2 SAM sites on Cuba during the crisis provided the CIA, together with the Oxcart planners, with an ideal opportunity for determining the sensitivity of the missile's radar receiver. For this particular operation, a US Navy destroyer based at Key West was equipped with one of the Palladium transmitters and positioned itself beyond the detection range of a Soviet early warning radar near Havana, its antenna protruding just above the horizon. Signals from the antenna then produced returns that appeared to be emanating from a US fighter, about to overfly Cuba. A US Navy submarine then surfaced near Havana Bay, just long enough to time-release a series of balloons carrying radar reflectors of varying sizes. The idea was that having detected the 'aircraft', the Soviets would switch on the SA-2 target-tracking radar, in

The North American F-108 Rapier was a proposed Improved Manned Interceptor (IMI). Spiralling costs eventually killed the programme, but its weapons systems were passed on to the YF-12A, their technology later proving invaluable in the failed F-111B and highly successful F-14 Tomcat programmes. (Rockwell International)

preparation for engaging the target. Release of the balloons, ahead of the original target, would produce a number of other returns; the smallest reported would present the highest level of radar sensitivity. The operation worked like clockwork and when a Cuban pilot told his ground controlled intercept (GCI) controller that he had acquired the 'intruder' on his radar, the technician on the destroyer flicked the switch and the 'fighter' disappeared!

After analysing all the intelligence data collected from this sortie and by other means, the CIA's Office of Scientific Intelligence (OSI), was able to conclude that Soviet radar capability would be able to track and 'lock-on' to the A-12, despite the aircraft's radar attenuating design features; however, undeterred, flight testing continued. A third Lockheed test pilot, Jim Eastham, was recruited into Oxcart, but still progress was slow due to technical problems, most of which were centred around the engines and Air Inlet Control System (AICS). In all it took 66 flights to push the speed envelope out from Mach 2.0 to Mach 3.2 and it was not until pneumatic pressure gauges, installed on the inlet systems to sense pressure variations of as little as 0.25 psi (0.02 bar), were replaced by an electrically controlled system from aircraft number nine (serial number '932) on, that the incidence of inlet disturbances was reduced.

YF-12

During December 1960, a separate project group working independently of the A-12 team, under Rus Daniell, was organised in the Skunk Works. From joint 715, (a point perpendicular to where the inboard wing leading edge meets the fuselage chine), the entire forward fuselage forebody of an A-12 was modified to create a Mach 3.2 interceptor. Originally designated AF-12, its 1,380-lb (627-kg) Hughes AN/ASG-18 pulse Doppler radar and 818-lb (371-kg) GAR-9 missile had been intended for the F-108 Rapier; however, following cancellation of the Rapier on 23 September 1959, DoD officials decided that development of its outstanding weapons system should continue on a 'stand alone' basis. Therefore Hughes continued research and development (R&D) work on both systems utilising a specially modified Convair B-58A Hustler (55-665, named *Snoopy 1*).

Kelly Johnson stands proudly beside the third and final AF-12 to be built, Article Number 1003, that first flew on 13 March 1964, with Bob Gilliland at the controls. (Lockheed Martin Skunk Works)

On 31 May 1960, the Air Force conducted a mock-up review of the AF-12 and was duly impressed. By June, AF-12 wind tunnel tests revealed directional stability problems resulting from the heavily revised nose profile and cockpit configuration. As a result a large folding fin was mounted under the aft fuselage, as were two shorter, fixed fins, beneath each nacelle. A bomber version of the A-12, designated RB-12, also reached the mock-up stage, but proved to be stillborn, as it represented too much of a threat to the highly political North American XB-70A Valkyrie. On 7 August 1963, Jim Eastham climbed aboard the interceptor prototype and took aircraft 60-6934 (the seventh A-12), for its first flight; a flight he would later modestly describe as a 'typical production test flight'.

On 24 May 1963, the programme received a temporary set-back when Agency pilot Ken Collins was forced to eject from A-12 60-6926, during a subsonic test flight. The subsequent crash occurred 14 miles (22.50-km) south of Wendover, Utah; a press cover story referred to the aircraft as being a Republic F-105 Thunderchief thus preserving security. An accident investigation established the cause of the incident to be a pitot-static system failure due to icing.

As 1963 drew to a close, the nine A-12s at Groom Lake had notched up a total of 573 flights totalling 765 hours. A year later, eleven A-12s had logged over 1,214 flights amounting to

To compensate for the YF-12's loss of directional stability due to the chine modifications necessary to house its infra-red detection system, two fixed dorsal fins on the underside of each engine nacelle and a large centreline folding fin were fitted. (Lockheed Martin Skunk Works)

1,669 hours – only 6 hours 23 minutes, however, was at Mach 3 and only 33 minutes at design speed, Mach 3.2.

Going public

As Oxcart grew in size and cost, concern was expressed within both the Agency and Air Force as to how much longer the programme could be kept a secret. It was also noted that technological data accumulated during the project would be of immense value if utilised in conjunction with 'white world' feasibility studies, then being conducted into supersonic passenger transport.

In November 1963, President Johnson was briefed on the programme, after which he directed that a formal announcement be prepared for release early in the New Year. Kelly Johnson noted in his diary, 'Plans going forward for surfacing of the AF-12 program. I worked on the draft to be used by President Johnson and proposed the terminology "A-11" as it was the non-anti-radar version.' On Saturday 29 February 1964, a few hours prior to the President announcing the existence of part of the programme, two AF-12s, 60-6934 and 60-6935 were flown from Area 51, to Edwards AFB, by Lou Schalk and Bob Gilliland, thereby diverting unwanted attention away from the 'blackworld' A-12 programme. At Edwards a 'buzz' had gone out to a few senior staff that something special might be happening on the first morning of their weekend off. In consequence, a few dozen

people witnessed the arrival of the extremely sleek interceptors, the like of which no one outside the programme had seen – except for a few desert dwellers and incredulous airline crews who occasionally reported sightings.

Lou Schalk recalls taxiing to their assigned hangar as eyes bulged and heads shook in utter disbelief. Unfortunately the arrival lost a touch of elegance when, to aid pushback into the hangar, they turned the aircraft through 180°. Lou recalls, 'This turnaround sent hot engine exhaust gases flooding into the hangar which caused the overhead fire extinguishers valves to open. These valves were big – like the flood valves on hangar decks of aircraft carriers – and the desert hadn't seen so much water since Noah's embarkation!'

Air Force 'baby'

Now subject of an Air Force programme, the aircraft's designation was changed to YF-12A to suit the USAF's nomenclature. The third YF-12A, 60-6936, soon joined the other two at Edwards and Jim Eastham continued the envelope expansion programme. Back at 'the Ranch' (Area 51), on 9 July 1964, Bill Park experienced a complete lock-up of his flight controls in aircraft 60-6939 as he descended for landing following a high-Mach flight. Despite trying to save the brand-new aircraft from rolling under while turning on to final approach, he could not stop the bank angle from increasing and was forced to eject. 'Punching out' at 200 kt (371 km/h) in a 34° bank, no more than 200 ft (61 m) above the ground, Park was very lucky to survive.

Yet another milestone in the programme was reached on 27 January 1965, when an A-12 flew a 2,580-mile (4152-km) sortie in one hour forty minutes, with three-quarters of the flight time spent at Mach 3.1. Then on 1 May 1965 (five years to the day that Gary Powers was shot down in his U-2), YF-12A 60-6936 seized back from the Soviet Union six World speed and altitude records. Fourteen days later, the Skunk Works received a contract for $500,000 for the production version of the interceptor, designated F-12B. However, no production go-ahead was given with the engineering contract. A further half-million dollars was granted on 10 November to keep basic F-12B design work alive. Similarly Hughes received $4.5 million to continue development of the AN/ASG-18 radar and fire control system.

On 29 March 1966, Kelly had a long meeting with Col Ben Bellis, Systems Project Officer (SPO), Hughes Aircraft Company and various members of the F-12 test force, during which he was asked to take on the task of integrating the weapons systems; this he agreed to do and fire control tests were continued. However, Secretary of Defense McNamara opposed production of the aircraft and as a result, on three occasions over the intervening two years, he denied the Air Force access to $90 million worth of funds which had been appropriated by Congress to begin F-12B production.

F-12B cancelled

Following a Senate Armed Services Committee hearing into the future of continental air defence, it was decided, in the light of intelligence

Upon retirement, on 24 July 1971, YF-12A serial 60-6936, Article Number 1003 was flown to the Air Force Museum at Wright-Patterson AFB, where it remains on permanent display as the sole survivor of its type. (USAF)

Initially, the remaining nine A-12 airframes were placed in hangar storage at Palmdale. (Lockheed Martin Skunk Works)

available at the time, to downgrade Aerospace Defense Command, which in turn rendered the F-12B unnecessary. On 5 January 1968, official notification was received from the US Air Force to 'close down the F-12B' and the YF-12A interceptor programme was formally ended on 1 February 1968. With the hindsight offered by post-Cold War knowledge of Soviet strategic bomber capabilities, this was probably a wise decision, but at the time seemed rash. It thus fell to the 'blackworld' Lockheed A-12 Oxcart programme to validate the concept of sustained high altitude, high-Mach flight in an operational environment.

Launch difficulties with the D-21 drone came to a head during the fourth launch, attempted from this aircraft, serial 60-6941, Article 135, on 30 July 1966. The drone, Number 504, collided with the mothership, which then pitched-up and disintegrated. Both Lockheed crewmembers successfully ejected, the pilot, Bill Park, survived, but the Launch Control Officer, Ray Torrick, drowned in the 'feet-wet' parachute landing, after the buoyancy aid in his suit failed to inflate. Kelly was so upset over the loss of one of his flight test staff that he cancelled further M-/D-21 test flights. (Lockheed Martin Skunk Works)

2. Technical Specification: Sensors

The SR-71 could be configured to carry three different types of reconnaissance-gathering sensors, enabling it to provide simultaneous, synoptic coverage of a wide range of data sources.

Cameras

There were five camera bays located in the underside of the SR-71's chine. In Bay C, a Fairchild F489 terrain objective camera (TROC) was mounted. This wide-angle mapping camera operated throughout the sortie, producing a single, overlapping exposure of the terrain below onto 35-mm film, which was 663 ft (202 m) in length. This provided approximately 15,500 nm (17,848 miles; 28724 km) of track coverage, allowing photo interpreters to cross-check the aircraft's position and provide additional ground cues in relation to targets photographed by the other sensors.

Next came two close-look Itek Corporation HR-308B technical objective cameras (TEOCs); mounted, in bays P and Q, they touted a maximum film capacity of 1,500 ft (457 m) and covered 2,000 nm (2,303 miles; 3706 km) of track. These narrow-field framing cameras produced multiple overlapping exposures of targets below or to either side of the aircraft's flight path and were activated either automatically, by the astro-inertial navigation system, or manually, by the RSO in the back seat.

Finally, two Hycon HR 9085 operational objective cameras (OOCs) were mounted in Bays S and T; these high-resolution, three-dimensional, panoramic cameras had a maximum film capacity of 3,300 ft (1006 m), which was sufficient to cover 3,600 frames, with alternate forward and aft exposures of the terrain below and to the side of the aircraft's track. Each camera had a lateral coverage of 45° and a total track coverage of about 1,500 nm (1,727 miles; 2780 km); the RSO manually operated these units.

On 5 April 1972, a new camera was added to the SR-71's payload, when a nose-mounted, optical bar camera (OBC), was operationally flight tested for the first time. This 'split scan' panoramic camera featured a 140° scan-head, fitted initially to a 24-in (61-cm) focal length lens. Also built by the Itek Corporation, it obtained high quality horizon-to-horizon imagery, by the full rotation of a prismatic optical barrel that swept above and below the aircraft's longitudinal axis. A frontally stabilised, mirrored scanning head bent light rays through 90° into the lens, which focused ground-target images by way of a second mirror through an exposure slit and onto the film at the cylindrical focal surface. Image/film synchronisation was split between the film, which was moved across the slit in one direction, and the exposure slit which travelled

'967 reveals the location and relative size of Bay Q. This was the home for either a TEOC or Elint-gathering equipment. (Paul F. Crickmore)

This image has been reproduced from a first-generation print from an OBC shot of Oakland baseball stadium taken during a routine US-based training sortie; note the outstanding clarity. (Paul F. Crickmore collection)

in the opposite direction, hence the term 'split scan'. This system allowed the SR-71 to photograph up to 100,000 square miles (2589975 km^2) of terrain per hour. The images were focused onto fine grain black-and-white film specially manufactured by Kodak, with an ISO rating of 8. Selected target images could be enlarged up to twenty times for photographic analysis and the system proved so successful that by the end of the year the Strategic Reconnaissance Center directed that the OBC should be used whenever weather over SEA permitted, and that on days of heavy cloud cover, a high resolution radar unit should be substituted; an operation that took maintenance

about 16 hours to complete. In November 1973, SAC received its first OBC unit fitted with a 30-in (76.2-cm) lens. This product produced a resolution of 10–12 in (25–30 cm) at nadir (directly below the aircraft) and having proved its worth, the OBC went on to replace the OOCs as a means of collecting panoramic coverage.

High Resolution Radar

The SR-71's detachable nose section could carry either the OBC, or a ground-mapping radar. The original high resolution radar (HRR), developed for the SR-71 was codenamed PIP (Product Improved Radar). Built by Loral, the radar's antenna received X-band-generated, doppler phase information, which was stored on a recorder housed in the forward right mission bay. This was then transferred onto a continuous, 4-in (10-cm) wide map film, via a ground-based optical correlator; the end result was an image, similar in appearance to that obtained by a camera, covering a strip of terrain 15 nm (17 miles; 28 km) wide and with a ground resolution of about 20 ft (6.10 m).

In 1973 the next generation SR-71 radar became operational. Known as the Capability Reconnaissance Radar (CAPRE); this improved HRR was manufactured by the Goodyear Aerospace Corporation and by 1980 the system had been improved to provide a resolution of 8 ft (2.44 m). CAPRE was replaced in 1983, by Loral's Advanced Synthetic Aperture Radar System (ASARS-1). This digitised high-definition, ground-mapping radar system provided a quantum leap in resolution of 2 ft (0.61 m) and its digitised format made near-real-time transmission a possibility.

EMR system

In May 1969, the SR-71's electromagnetic reconnaissance system (EMR), was deployed for operations. Activated by the RSO, this passive collection system conducted a general search between 30 MHz and 40 GHz. When a signal of interest matched the characteristics of those stored on the EMR's computer, it was automatically isolated by a receiver enabling a detector to record such details as frequency, amplitude, pulse width, pulse repetition frequency and relative bearing, onto a magnetic tape which also logged signal capture time.

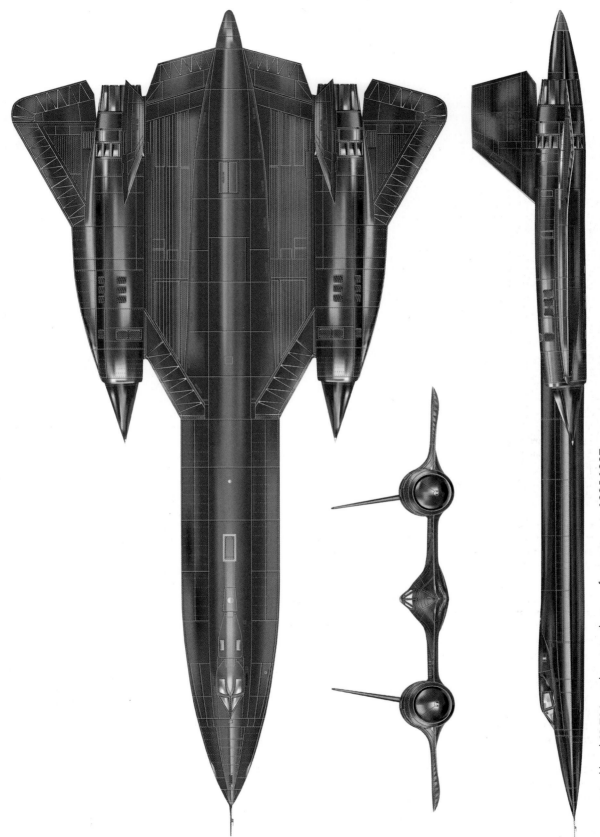

Lockheed SR-71A, at the reintroduction of operations in 1995-1997

Operating simultaneously in two modes, the EMR conducted both a general and special signal search; however, when priority intelligence was required, the system defaulted to the latter.

In April 1972, a new Elint recording system was deployed to Kadena for operational testing; known as the Ampex-1700, it made simultaneous analogue recordings of radar signals in more than one band, which made possible a more detailed analysis of signal characteristics. Having proved its worth, it too was incorporated as an update on the rest of the fleet a year later.

Defensive Electronic System

Another of the more sensitive areas on the SR-71 was undoubtedly its highly effective defensive electronic system (DEF). The key to the SR-71's survival in hostile or 'denied airspace' was its high speed and extreme altitude capabilities. To successfully intercept the aircraft, an SA-2 would need to be fired some 30 miles (48 km) ahead of its target. With the crew alerted to a SAM launch via the passive radar homing and warning receiver (RHAWR), a slight adjustment in the SR-71's course, altitude and speed would usually be sufficient to upset the missile's ability to re-calculate the intercept solution and steer itself in the rarefied air to the target's newly calculated position. However, for additional insurance,

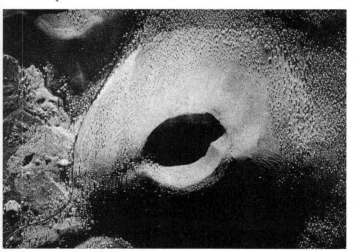

This stunning shot of Sunset crater was the first ASARS-1 radar image taken from an SR-71 to be released. (Goodyear)

should the aircraft be forced to descend to lower altitudes during any inflight emergencies, it was equipped with a DEF system which was continually updated to ensure that it was kept abreast of the latest anti-aircraft developments. The initial operational suite was obliquely referred to by SAC as Systems A to D, but in March 1969, System E became operational and this was followed in June 1970 by System F. Two years later, in April 1972, a Special Elint Beacon Receiver (SEBER), known as System G, was deployed for operational testing and was later deployed on the rest of the fleet; this unit was designed specifically to collect the beacon transponder signals of SA-2 SAMs.

Each system was in turn updated and became DEF A2, C2, H and M; by the time the platform was first retired in 1990, a system utilising programmable software had become fully operational, known as DEF A2C, it was capable of defeating all known threats.

Data Processing: The Achilles heel

It had long been acknowledged within the Senior Crown programme, that in order to compete with reconnaissance-gathering satellites in the battle to procure operational funding from an ever-diminishing defence budget, the SR-71 Blackbird desperately required a data link. Research and development funds were used to develop and install the long overdue system during the 1994/95 programme reactivation. Manufactured by C3 Com, of Salt Lake City, the data link's antenna was housed in a small radome, just forward of the front undercarriage well. A digital cassette recorder system (DCRsi) provided recording and playback of both Elint and ASARS data. Near-real-time data was provided if the aircraft was within 300 nm (345 miles; 555 km) line-of-sight range of a receiving station; if not, the entire recorded collection could be downloaded in ten minutes, once within station range.

The next sensor enhancement took place during 1997/98, with the development of an electro-optical back-plate for the TEOCs. Manufactured by Recon Optical, located in Barrington, Illinois, these digitised units replaced film, thereby facilitating the transmission of high quality, close-look imagery, via the data link, in near-real time, directly to theatre commanders.

3. Operational History: A-12 and Early SR-71 Operations

On 5 August 1965, under the codename Skylark, Gen. Marshall S. Carter, director of the National Security Agency, ordered that Oxcart achieve emergency operational readiness by 5 November, to cover Cuba – this was achieved, albeit on a limited basis, but no sorties were ever flown.

Stateside air-refuelling operations with the A-12 continued to be routinely conducted by tankers of the 903rd ARS, but in order to provide strategic reach for possible global A-12 operations, PF-1 fuel was pre-positioned to Eielson AFB, Alaska; Thule in Greenland, Kadena on the island of Okinawa, Japan and Incirlik, Turkey. Despite this and the Arab-Israeli Six Day War of June 1967, Oxcart was not deployed.

The fact is that the 1 May shoot-down of Gary Powers and his U-2 generated enormous reservations about the political acceptability of manned overflight reconnaissance missions. The question therefore was what should be done with this multi-million dollar, national security asset? One possible short-term answer appeared to be in a classified project, codenamed Upwind.

In 1964, KH-4 Corona satellite imagery revealed what some analysts feared were anti-ballistic missiles, located at Tallinn in Estonia. However, the resolution of satellite, or 'overhead' imagery available at that time was not capable of producing the required level of detail to resolve the ensuing debate. To settle the issue, the Office of Special Activities (OSA) proposed that a composite mission be flown, consisting of an A-12 equipped with a high-resolution camera, and a U-2 configured for gathering Elint. The A-12 would fly from the United States into the Baltic Sea, where it would rendezvous with the U-2 thereafter, the former would proceed north of Norway, and then south, along the Soviet-Finnish border. Just before reaching Leningrad, the A-12 would head west-southwest, down the Baltic Sea, skirting the coasts of Estonia, Latvia, Lithuania, Poland and East Germany before heading back west, to the United States. The 11,000-mile (17703-km) flight would take 8 hours 40 minutes to complete and require four air refuellings. Although not violating Soviet airspace, it was hoped that the high-speed, high-altitude target would provoke Soviet radar operators into activating the Tallinn system. The A-12, with its Type 1 camera, would secure high resolution imagery of the Tallinn site and the more vulnerable U-2 would be standing off, beyond the range of SAMs, recording the Soviet radar's signal characteristics. Both Agency and Defense Department officials supported the proposal; however, Secretary of State Dean Rusk strongly opposed it and so the influential 303 Committee never forwarded it to President Johnson for his approval.

During the course of a meeting held on 22 March 1965, between Brig. Gen. Jack Ledford (the CIA/USAF liaison officer) and Secretary of Defense (Sec Def) Cyrus Vance, it was agreed to grant $3.7 million to provide support facilities at Kadena for the possible deployment of 'Cygnus' (as the A-12 was nicknamed) aircraft under a project codenamed *Black Shield*. On 3 June 1965, Secretary McNamara consulted the Under

Aircraft 60-6932, Article 129, was one of only three A-12s to ever fly an operational mission. It was lost during an FCF, prior to being re-deployed back to the United States, on 5 June 1968. Jack Weeks, the aircraft's pilot, was killed. (CIA)

Secretary of the Air Force about the build-up of SA-2s around Hanoi and the possibility of substituting the more vulnerable U-2s with A-12s to conduct recce flights over the North Vietnamese capital. He was informed that once adequate aircraft performance was validated, *Black Shield* could be cleared to go.

Four A-12s were selected for *Black Shield* operations, Kelly Johnson taking personal responsibility for ensuring that the aircraft were completely 'squawk-free' (without technical problems). Additionally, in order to further prove the mission readiness of the system, on 20 November 1965 a Cygnus aircraft completed a maximum endurance flight of 6 hours 20 minutes, during which it reached speeds above Mach 3.2 and altitudes approaching 90,000 ft (27432 m). On 2 December, the 303 Committee received the first of many proposals to deploy Oxcart to the Far East. However, the proposal was rejected, as were several other submissions that were made throughout 1966.

In May 1967, the National Security Council was briefed that North Vietnam was about to receive surface-to-surface ballistic missiles. If true, this would represent a serious escalation of the conflict and one that would certainly require hard evidence to substantiate. Consequently President Johnson was briefed on the threat, and DCI Richard Helms again proposed that the 303 Committee authorise deployment of Oxcart, as it was ideally equipped to carry missions to verify the existence of the missile threat, having a

On 26 June 1968, the five surviving members of the 1129th Special Activities Squadron that had taken the secret A-12 into battle were each awarded the coveted CIA Intelligence Star for Valour. (Paul F. Crickmore collection)

superior speed and altitude capability to both the U-2 and pilotless drones, as well as a better camera. President Johnson approved the plan and in mid-May an airlift was begun to establish *Black Shield* at Kadena AB.

At 08:00 on 22 May 1967, Mele Vojvodich deployed A-12 60-6937 from Area 51 to Okinawa during a flight that lasted 6 hours 6 minutes and included three air refuellings. Two days later Jack Layton joined him in 60-6930, and 60-6932, flown by Jack Weeks, arrived on Okinawa on 27 May, having been forced to divert into Wake Island for a day, following INS and radio problems. The detachment was declared ready for operations on 29 May and following weather reconnaissance flights on the 30th, it was

Right: This chart was used by Frank Murray on 21 June 1968, during the final A-12 flight (made in Article 131) from Area 51 to Palmdale's storage facility.

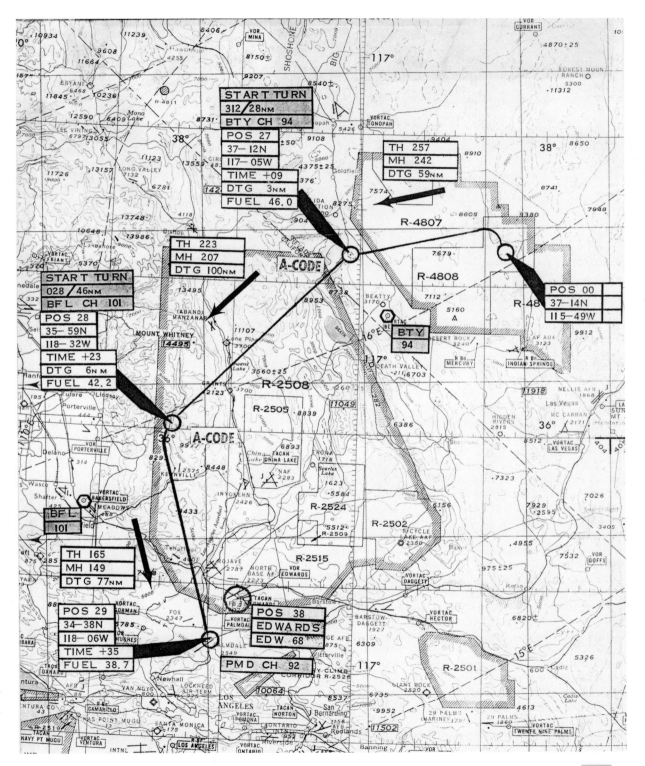

START TURN
312/28NM
BTY CH 94
POS 27
37—12N ±50
117—05W
TIME +09
DTG 3NM
FUEL 46.0

TH 257
MH 242
DTG 59NM

TH 223
MH 207
DTG 100NM

A-CODE

POS 00
37—14N
115—49W

START TURN
028/46NM
BFL CH 101
POS 28
35—59N
118—32W
TIME +23
DTG 6NM
FUEL 42.2

BTY
94

A-CODE

BFL
101

TH 165
MH 149
DTG 77NM

POS 29
34—38N
118—06W
TIME +35
FUEL 38.7

POS 38
EDWARDS
EDW 68

PMD CH 92

Before final disposal, the A-12s were moved outside. All nine survivors are seen here, having had protective coatings applied. (Lockheed Martin Skunk Works)

determined that conditions were ideal for an A-12 camera run over North Vietnam; Project Headquarters in Washington then placed *Black Shield* on alert for its first operational mission. Avionics specialists checked various systems and sensors, and at 16:00 Mele Vojvodich and back-up pilot Jack Layton attended a mission alert briefing. At 22:00 (twelve hours before the planned take-off time) a review of the weather confirmed the mission was still on, so the pilots went to bed to ensure they got a full eight hours of 'crew rest'.

They awoke on the morning of 31 May, to torrential rain – a new phenomenon to the 'desert dwelling' A-12s. However, meteorological conditions over 'the collection area' were good and at 08:00, Kadena received a final clearance from Washington that *Black Shield* flight X001 was a 'go'. On cue, Mele engaged both afterburners and made the first instrument-guided take-off of an A-12. A few minutes later he burst through cloud and flew 60-6937 up to 25,000 ft (7620 m) to top-off its tanks from a waiting KC-135. Having disengaged from the '135's boom, he accelerated and climbed to operational speed and altitude, having informed

Kadena ('home-plate') that aircraft systems were running as per the book and the back-up services of Jack Layton would not be required. He penetrated hostile airspace at Mach 3.2 and 80,000 ft (24384 m) during a so-called 'front door' entry over Haiphong, then continuing over Hanoi before exiting North Vietnam near Dien Bien Phu. A second air refuelling took place over Thailand, followed by another climb to altitude before making a second penetration of North Vietnamese airspace near the Demilitarised Zone (DMZ); after which he recovered the aircraft after three instrument approaches in driving rain, back at Kadena. In all, the flight had lasted 3 hours 40 minutes, several SA-2s were fired at the aircraft but all detonated above and well behind their target – a fact confirmed by the pilot, despite recent assertions that such an event failed to occur until a mission some months later.

The 'photo-take' was downloaded and sent by a special courier aircraft to the Eastman Kodak plant in Rochester, New York for processing, after which it was discovered that '937s large Type 1 camera had successfully photographed ten priority target categories including 70 of the 190 known SAM sites. By mid July, A-12 over-flights had determined with a high degree of confidence that there were no surface-to-surface missiles in North Vietnam; however, such

After the spy ship USS *Pueblo* had been captured by North Korea, an A-12 mission was launched on 25 January 1965 in an attempt to find it. Technical failure caused Jack Weeks to abort this first mission, but Frank Murray had more luck the next day, bringing back this image of Wonsan. (National Archive via Tim Brown)

Jim Eastham, in a Lockheed F-104 Starfighter, trailed Bob Gilliland down Palmdale's runway during the maiden flight of the SR-71 on 22 December 1964. Eastham flew chase for the first sortie, ensuring that Gilliland was aware of everything happening outside his aircraft, as well as in. (Lockheed Martin Skunk Works)

Shortly after topping-off the fuel tanks of his SR-71A, Bill Weaver accelerated and climbed to altitude, where the aircraft broke-up at high speed. A-12 and Early SR operations were serviced by KC-135Qs with discrete fuel systems to keep the tanker's own fuel separate to that of the Blackbirds. All of the KC-135Qs were converted from -135A standard, this machine retaining the original short fin and rudder. (Lockheed Martin Skunk Works)

reconnaissance flights soon became invaluable, as they provided timely information to mission planners as to which SA-2 sites were occupied, as well as high quality post-strike bomb damage assessment (BDA) imagery.

During sortie number BX6732, flown by Denny Sullivan on 28 October 1967, the pilot received indications on his Radar Homing and Warning Receiver (RHAWR), of almost continuous radar activity focused on his A-12, whilst he was both inbound and outbound, over North Vietnam; in addition, a single SA-2 was launched. Two days later, during sortie BX6734, Sullivan was again flying high over North Vietnam when two SAM sites tracked him on his first pass. On his second pass, while approaching Hanoi from the East, he again noted that he was being tracked on radar; then, over the next few minutes he counted no less than eight SA-2 detonations in 'the general area though none particularly close' – this was the first occasion that the North Vietnamese had employed a salvo launch technique against the A-12. After recovering the aircraft back at Kadena without further incident, a post-flight inspection revealed that a tiny piece of shrapnel had penetrated the lower wing fillet of Sullivan's

aircraft and become lodged against the support structure of the wing tank – history would prove this to be the only enemy 'damage' inflicted on a Lockheed 'Blackbird'.

During 1967, a total of 41 A-12 missions was alerted, of which 22 were actually granted approval for flight. Between 1 January and 31 March, 1968, some 17 missions were alerted, of which seven were flown, five over North Vietnam and two over North Korea. The latter two came about following seizure, on the night of 23/24 January 1968, of the USS *Pueblo* – a US Navy Signals Intelligence (Sigint) vessel, by North Korea. The first sortie was attempted by Jack Weeks on 25 January, but a malfunction on the A-12 resulted in an abort shortly after take-off. The next day Frank Murray completed the task during mission BX6847, as he now recalls, 'I left Kadena, topped-off, then entered northern airspace over the Sea of Japan via the Korean Straits. My first pass started off near Vladivostok, then with the camera on, I flew over the east coast of North Korea where we thought the boat was. As I approached Wonsan I could see the *Pueblo* through my view sight. The harbour was all iced up except at the very entrance and there she was, sitting off to the right of the main entrance. I continued west before completing a 180° turn and flew back again over North Korea. I made a total of three passes over 'denied territory', photographing the whole of North Korea from the DMZ to the Yalu river. As far as I know, I was undetected throughout the flight, but when I got back to Kadena intell. [intelligence] told me that the Chinese had detected me and told the North Koreans, but they never reacted.' Back at Kadena the 'take' was unloaded and flown to Yakota Air Base, Japan where the 67th Reconnaissance Technical Squadron (RTS) had been activated to enable the more timely exploitation of such data by theatre commanders.

On 8 May 1968, Jack Layton successfully completed mission BX6858 over North Korea; it was to prove the final operational A-12 flight. A long standing debate concerning whether the A-12 or a programme known as Senior Crown should carry forward the manned strategic reconnaissance baton, had, after three years been resolved and Oxcart, after completing just 29 operational sorties, was vanquished. In early March 1968, the 'new kids on the block' began arriving at Kadena to take over the *Black Shield* commitment. Those A-12s back at 'the Area' were flown to Palmdale and placed in storage by 7 June. At Kadena the three aircraft that had performed all the *Black Shield* missions were

readied for a return transpacific ferry flight. On 5 June 1968, however, a final tragedy hit the Oxcart programme, when Jack Weeks was killed during a functional check flight (FCF), in Article Number 129. The aircraft and its pilot were lost without trace in the Pacific Ocean. The two remaining A-12s on Okinawa, Articles 127 and 131 were ferried back to Area 51, before being flown to Palmdale, the last flight being made by Frank Murray on 21 June 1968, in Article 131.

Senior Crown

Whilst working on Oxcart back in the early spring of 1962, Kelly had mentioned the possibility of producing a variant of the aircraft for the Air Force. Duly, Lockheed was issued with a 90-day study contract, wherein various Air Force mission options were identified and defined in terms of the A-12 platform. By the end of April 1962, two different mock-ups were under construction, the R-12 (a pure reconnaissance platform), and the RS-12 (a reconnaissance/strike variant). On 18 February 1963, Lockheed received pre-contractual authority to build six aircraft on the understanding that a further twenty-five aircraft would be ordered by 1 July. Col Leo Geary had been the RS-12 System Program Officer (SPO), but after a protracted debate, it was decided that the A-12 project group, under Col Templeton, would inherit the R-12, which became

The third SR-71 to be written-off was '954, the aircraft suffering a wheel failure during a maximum gross weight take-off at Edwards AFB, on 11 April 1969. Lockheed allocated its own Article Numbers to individual airframes, while the Air Force applied standard serial numbers. Thus, 64-17954 was Article Number 2005 to Lockheed. (Lockheed Martin Skunk Works)

The first SR-71 to be written-off was '952. The aircraft was flying a test mission from Edwards on 25 January 1966 when it broke up at high speed and crashed near Tucumcari, New Mexico. Bill Weaver (left) confounded the accident investigators by his amazing Mach-3 escape, but his back-seater, Jim Zwayer, was killed in the accident. (both Lockheed Martin Skunk Works)

designated SR-71 by the Air Force and was given the programme codename Senior Crown. The RS-12 and later the B-12/B-71 proposals for a strike version of the aircraft would fail to win production contracts despite Kelly having demonstrated to the Air Force the unique capabilities of such a platform – a fact largely due to the far greater lobbying powers of the XB-70 and later FB-111 fraternity. In a speech made on 24 July 1964, President Johnson revealed to the world the existence of the SR-71.

In August, Kelly phoned Bob Murphy and asked him if he wanted to work on the SR-71 programme. At the time, Murphy was a superintendent in charge of D-21 drone

production. Drone Number One was undergoing final checkout while nine others were at various stages of assembly. Bob accepted the offer and was immediately briefed by Kelly who said, 'I want you to go to Palmdale and get Site 2 away from Rockwell. Hire the people you need. The pieces of the SR-71 will be up with you on November 1st and I want her flying before Christmas. Oh, I also want you to move up there because I don't want you to commute.' Rockwell controlled all three sites at Palmdale, using Sites 1 and 3 for XB-70 construction; Site 2 housed a paint shop, telephone exchange and other facilities. Following a meeting with the base commander and various Rockwell representatives, 'Murph' successfully managed to gain control of Site 2 for Lockheed. The prototype SR-71A, serial 64-17950 (Article Number 2001 – it was given this particular number by Kelly, as he believed that the performance of the platform was such that it would be invulnerable to interception until at least that date), was delivered from Burbank to

Site 2, Air Force Plant 42, Building 210, at Palmdale for final assembly on 29 October, by two large trailers specifically designed for the task. At that point Bob Murphy's team 'went into overdrive' in an attempt to fulfil the extremely tight deadline set by Kelly. Earlier that year, Kelly had promoted the charismatic Robert J. Gilliland to the position of Chief Project Pilot for the SR-71; a post for which he was eminently qualified, having gained a great deal of experience as a member of the F-104 and A-12 flight test teams. Bob worked closely with Dick Miller who led the flight test engineering effort for the entire contractor test programme, as it was Miller's responsibility to implement specific tests to be completed on individual flights.

Flight Testing

With two J58s installed, '950 conducted its first engine test run on 18 December 1964. Three days later, a 'non-flight' was conducted where Gilliland accelerated the aircraft to 120 kt (138 mph; 222 km/h) before snapping the throttles back to idle and deploying the large 40-ft (12-m) diameter drag 'chute.

On 22 December 1964, Gilliland (using his personal callsign DUTCH 51) got airborne from Runway 25 at Palmdale in '950. The back seat, or Reconnaissance Systems Officer's (RSO's) position, remained empty on this historic flight for safety reasons. After take-off Bob immediately retracted the landing gear, reduced afterburners to 'min', turned right and continued his climb northbound over Edwards test range until he levelled off at 20,000 ft (6096 m) and 0.9 Mach. Jim Eastham was flying chase in one of three F-104s, the other two being flown by USAF test pilots Col Robert 'Fox' Stephens and Lt Col Walt Daniels. Eastham tucked his F-104 into close formation on '950's right wing, while both pilots calibrated and verified accurate pitot-static-derived flight data. A series of handling checks was then flown during which the aircraft's static and dynamic stability was assessed. These checks were carried out with the Stability Augmentation System (SAS) axes switched 'on' and 'off', both 'individually' and 'collectively'. Performance comparisons of predicted values of speed versus thrust and fuel consumption were also recorded, followed by a climb to 30,000 ft (9144 m) where cabin pressure,

Both pilot Lt Col Bill Skliar and RSO, Maj. Noel Warner, were lucky to escape unhurt when '954 suffered a take-off accident (above). The aircraft's dark paint scheme hides the extent of the damage caused by the conflagration when 80,000 lb (36287 kg) of JP-7 went up in flames (left). Unlike the A-12, the SR-71 was able to burn JP-7 fuel which, while still requiring a specialised tanker, allowed a less weighty fuel system to be installed in the KC-135Q. (both USAF)

oxygen flow and temperature control were checked. Having passed Mojave, Gilliland turned left, to head west, before completing a 180° turn to the left and rolling out on a southerly track over the Sierra Nevadas.

As all systems were performing well, it was time to complete a supersonic dash. So with Jim sticking to the 'SR' like glue, Bob eased the two throttles into 'min burner', scanned engine parameters and slid the throttles up to 'max'. The light test jet accelerated very rapidly to 400 kt (461 mph; 741 km/h) in level flight and then on up to supersonic speed. At Mach 1.4 Bob's attention was drawn to the flashing of the 'Master Caution' warning lights. A glance at the annunciator panel identified the problem as 'Canopy Unsafe'. Visually checking the two

canopy locking hooks, Bob verified that the canopy was 'fully locked'. The pressure-sensitive micro-switch that transmitted the electrical 'unsafe' signal, had been triggered by an aerodynamic low pressure area above the aircraft, which had sucked the canopy up, against the locking hooks. In reality the canopy remained locked, and having analysed the situation as safe, Bob advanced the throttles once again, continuing his acceleration and climb while closely scanning the instruments. On reaching 50,000 ft (15240 m) and Mach 1.5, he eased the throttles out of burner into 'mil' position and began to decelerate to 350 kt (403 mph; 649 km/h) indicated airspeed, after which he descended to 20,000 ft (6096 m) to allow the engines to cool down.

Approaching Palmdale, Bob was advised by Test Ops that Kelly had requested a subsonic flyby down the runway. Happy to comply, Bob and the accompanying '104s streaked by to highlight the successful completion of the first flight. Downwind with the gear down and locked he turned '950 onto a wide base leg and set-up a long final approach at 185 kt (213 mph; 343 km/h). Touching down smoothly on Palmdale's Runway 25 he gently lowered the nose and deployed the drag 'chute. At 50 kt (58 mph; 93 km/h) the 'chute was jettisoned, the aircraft was turned off the active runway and taxied back towards the crowd of USAF dignitaries, Lockheed engineers and technicians who awaited Bob's debriefing.

After congratulations from Kelly Johnson and the others, Bob narrated details of his first flight chronologically from engine start-up to shut-down. Clarifying questions were then fielded by some of the technicians, after which a typescript of the recorded briefing was circulated to all

concerned. Further details were gathered, for later dissemination, from cockpit-mounted camera recordings and their 'automatic observer' panels. Aircraft '951 and '952 were soon added to the test fleet for contractor development of payload systems and shortly after the Phase II Developmental Test Program was started, four other Lockheed test pilots were brought into the project: Jim Eastham, Bill Weaver, Art Peterson and Darrell Greenamyer.

Developmental efforts within Lockheed were matched by those of Air Force Systems Command (AFSC), where Col Ben Bellis had been appointed the SR-71 SPO. His task was to structure a 'Development and Evaluation Program' that would evaluate the new aircraft for the Air Force. This programme was undertaken by the SR-71/YF-12 Test Force at the Air Force Flight Test Center, Edwards AFB. Both

As a very-high-performing aircraft which pushed contemporary technology to its limits, it was inevitable that the SR-71 would suffer losses, especially during its test phase. In the majority of accidents a cause could usually be identified and steps taken to avoid such a problem arising again. Nevertheless, the precise circumstances surrounding the loss of 64-17953, Article Number 2004, on 18 December 1965 remain a mystery to this day. (Lockheed Martin Skunk Works)

Phase I 'Experimental' and Phase II 'Development' test flying had moved to Edwards where SR-71As '953, '954, and '955 were to be evaluated by the 'blue suiters'. On 18 November and 18 December 1965, the two SR-71B pilot trainers, '956 and '957, successfully completed their first flights; but the SR-71s were plagued by problems associated with their electrical systems, tank sealing and with reaching design range.

While these problems were being worked at, Beale AFB (chosen home for the newcomer) had been undergoing an $8.4-million construction programme, which included the installation of an army of specialised technical support facilities. The 4200th Strategic Reconnaissance Wing was activated at Beale on 1 January 1965; three months latter, four support squadrons were formed. In January 1966, Col Doug Nelson was appointed commander of the new wing, a job he was well qualified for, having been the Director of Operations for Oxcart. Doug began by selecting a small group of highly competent sub-commanders and Strategic Air Command (SAC) fliers to form the initial cadre of the SR-71 unit. Col Bill Hayes became the Deputy Commander for maintenance, Lt Col Ray Haupt Chief Instructor pilot, Col Walt Wright commanded the Medical Group, Col Clyde Deaniston supervised all Category III flight test planning and the flight

crews were recruited from the best SAC bomber pilots and navigators in the service. The first two of eight Northrop T-38 Talons had arrived at Beale on 7 July 1965; these would be used as 'companion trainers' to maintain overall flying proficiency for SR-71 crews, at a fraction of the cost of flying the main aircraft. On 7 January 1966 Col Doug Nelson and his Chief Instructor, Lt Col Ray Haupt delivered the first SR-71B to Beale AFB; five months later on 14 April, Nelson and Maj. Al Pennington took delivery of Beale's first SR-71A, serial 64-17958. On 25 June 1966, the 4200th was re-designated the 9th Strategic Reconnaissance Wing (SRW), its component flying squadrons being the 1st and 99th Strategic Reconnaissance Squadrons (SRS), and crew training together with Category III Operational Testing proceeded in earnest.

Test Force Losses

The first SR-71 loss occurred on 25 January 1966, when Bill Weaver and his test engineer, Jim Zwayer took off from Edwards in SR-71A '952. The main objectives of the flight were to evaluate navigation and reconnaissance systems, and investigate procedures for improving high-Mach cruise performance by reducing trim drag, thereby lowering fuel burn and increasing range. This research required the centre of gravity (CG) be moved further aft than normal, to compensate

Not all of the test fleet suffered accidents. Aircraft '955 was the test force workhorse and was operated extensively by AF Logistics Command from Plant 42, Palmdale. It remained in service, exclusively on test operations, until 1985. (USAF)

Formation flying was not one of the SR-71's neater tricks, especially with something as slow as a U-2. Here, Kelly Johnson's 'dynamic duo' was photographed while briefly occupying the same piece of sky during a one-off photocall. The SR-71A flew the ASARS-1 trials for the Blackbird fleet, while the U-2R was the test bird for that type's ASARS-2 system. (Lockheed Martin Skunk Works)

for the rearward shift of the aerodynamic centre-of-pressure at high Mach. After in-flight refuelling, DUTCH 64 climbed back to cruising altitude. While in a 15° right banked turn, manually controlling the right forward bypass doors at Mach 3.17 and at 77–78,000 ft (23470–23774 m), Weaver experienced a right inlet unstart. Bank angle immediately increased from 35° to 60° and the aircraft entered a pitch-up that exceeded the restorative authority of the flight controls and SAS. The aircraft disintegrated but miraculously Weaver survived, although Jim Zwayer was tragically killed in the incident. The excessive trim drag problem was rectified by Kelly, who designed a 'wedge', that was inserted between the aircraft's forward fuselage and its detachable nose section. This moved the centre of lift forward, thus reducing static margin and trim drag. The external result was a distinctive 2° nose-up tilt.

The SR-71 prototype was written off on 10 January 1967, during an anti-skid brake system evaluation at Edwards AFB. The Lockheed test pilot, Art Peterson, escaped with a cracked disc in his back.

The next test force aircraft to be lost was '954, during the course of a maximum gross-weight take-off from Edwards on 11 April 1969. Shortly after rotation, the aircraft suffered a wheel failure, debris penetrated the fuel tanks which in turn triggered a fuel fire. Lt Col Bill Skliar and his RSO, Maj. Noel Warner, managed to bring the aircraft to a halt on the long runway and escape unhurt. On 18 December 1969, test force Director Lt Col Joe Rogers, together with RSO Lt Col Gary Heidelbaugh, experienced an explosion while accelerating after air refuelling. They decelerated, but continued to suffer control difficulties; shortly thereafter '953 entered a pitch-up, forcing both crewmembers to eject. They were unhurt, as the aircraft came down at the southern end of Death Valley. To this day the cause of the explosion remains unknown.

Beale Losses

Beale lost its first aircraft, SR-71A '966, on 13 April 1967, following a night air refuelling incident. It was Capt. Earle Boone's ninth training sortie and he was flying with Capt. 'Butch' Sheffield, as his regular RSO had a cold,

Shortly after 14:00 on Friday, 7 January 1966, the 9th SRW commander, Col Doug Nelson, together with Ray Haupt, delivered the first SR-71 trainer, serial '956, to Beale AFB. Four T-38 Talons were in attendance for this flyby, the Northrop trainers being used by the SR crews for continuation training. (Paul F. Crickmore collection)

which prevented him from passing the pre-flight medical. After leaving the tanker, Earle turned to avoid thunderstorms that straddled his planned acceleration to climb track. As he climbed, prior to performing the 'dipsy doodle' manoeuvre, designed to reduce fuel consumption during transonic breakthrough, he suffered a series of engine stalls and his airspeed drifted down to 170 kt (196 mph; 315 km/h) at 37,000 ft (11278 m). Heavy with fuel, the jet shuddered in a stall; Earle fought hard to regain control, but '966 suddenly entered a pitch-up rotation from which there was no recovery. Fortunately, both men safely ejected as '966 fell to earth not far from where Bill Weaver's aircraft had crashed in northern New Mexico.

On the night of 25 October 1967, a black-tie dinner was being held at the Beale Officers' club with Kelly Johnson as guest of honour. At the same time, Maj. Roy St Martin and Capt. John

Carnochan were flying a night sortie in aircraft '965. As Roy eased the aircraft into the descent profile over central Nevada, the gyro-stabilised reference platform for the Astro-inertial Navigation System (ANS) drifted without a failure warning. Since this was the source for providing attitude reference signals to the primary flight instruments and guidance information to the autopilot, the aircraft entered an increasing right bank, while the Flight Director and the Atitude Director Indicator instruments displayed no deviation from wing-level flight. At 20:25, in the autumn at high altitude over Nevada, there was no visual horizon for external reference. The aircraft rolled over, the nose fell far below a safe descent angle and plunged through 60,000 ft (18288 m). The crew sensed something was wrong when Roy glanced at the standby artificial horizon (a small instrument awkwardly positioned low in the cockpit) and was alarmed to see it indicate a 'screaming dive and roll-over toward inverted flight'. He attempted a 'recovery from unusual positions manoeuvre', and managed to roll the wings level, but roaring through 40,000 ft (12192 m) well above the speed from which level flight could be achieved, both the men had to eject. The RSO went first, full into a Mach 1.4 slipstream and just as Roy ejected he heard the warning horn that the aircraft was now below 10,000 ft (3048 m)! Aircraft '965 plunged into the ground near Lovelock, Nevada like a

Of the two SR-71Bs delivered to the 9th SRW for pilot training, the second, serial '957, was lost on 11 January 1968. 'Gray' Sowers and Dave Fruehauf both ejected safely, but the SR-71B fleet never really recovered. A second trainer was produced by adding the forward fuselage from a static-test SR-71 to the wings and rear fuselage of a YF-12A, but the resulting aircraft was disliked and seldom flown. (Appeal Democrat)

hypervelocity meteorite. Luckily both men survived without permanent injuries. Following an accident board of investigation, several instrument changes were implemented on the fleet together with an amended training programme that contained reduced night flights until crews had accumulated more daytime experience in the SR-71.

As the 9th SRW approached the time for overseas deployment much talk in the crew lounge was devoted to anti-SAM tactics. The plan was to penetrate enemy airspace at Mach 3. If fired upon, the pilot would accelerate to Mach 3.2 and climb, thereby forcing the missile's guidance system to recalculate the intercept solution. One 'half-baked' idea was to also dump fuel to become lighter, thereby increasing climb-rate; but a crew ended the debate during a sortie over Montana by dumping fuel for ten seconds to see if the afterburner would ignite the fuel trail. Instead this turned instantly into an ice cloud in the frigid -55°C stratosphere and left a 5-mile (8-km) long contrail-finger pointing directly at the aircraft. The pilot reported that he could see the trail for hundreds of miles after having turned back towards the west!

During this work-up period, yet another incident befell the 9th SRW, on 11 January 1968.

Lt Col 'Gray' Sowers and 'student' Capt. Dave Fruehauf, on his third training sortie, experienced a double generator failure in SR-71B '957, near Spokane, Washington. They immediately switched off all non-essential electrically powered equipment to conserve battery power and made repeated attempts to re-set both generators, which would come on briefly only to fail again. With most of the bases in Washington State unsuitable for diversion, the crew hoped to make Portland, Oregon, only to discover that they were weathered out. They had little option therefore but to press on for Beale. Their long, straight-in approach looked good until the 175 kt (202 mph; 324 km/h) 'final' placed the aircraft in its natural 10° nose-up angle of attack. This allowed some dry-tank fuel inlet ports to 'draw in air' that in turn interrupted the gravity flow of fuel to the engine combustion chambers because the fuel boost pumps were inoperative. The resulting cavitation caused both J58s to flame out and at 3,000 ft (914 m) Gray ordered bail-out. Both crewmembers survived as '957 'pancaked' inverted only 7 miles (11 km) north of Beale's long runway.

Rolling down Beale's Runway 14 in '977, in October 1968 were new pilot/RSO team Majs

It is a lasting testament to the genius of Kelly Johnson that his influence affected so many Lockheed designs, usually targeted at massively disparate roles. Here a T-33 trainer poses with an SR-71A. This particular Blackbird, '965, was the second operational aircraft to be lost by the 9th SRW. It crashed during the evening of 10 June 1966. (USAF)

Abe Kardong and Jim Kogler. Approaching V1 (rotate speed, i.e. the speed at which the nosewheel leaves the runway) a wheel failed, throwing shrapnel into the fuel cells causing a fuel fire. Abe aborted take-off at high speed which caused the remaining tyres on that leg to burst. The brake 'chute blossomed only to be consumed by the fire. With one wing low and the aircraft off centre to the runway, '977's sharp

inlet spike knifed through the barrier cable at the end of the runway, rendering it useless. Now on the overrun, Jim ejected while Abe rode out the high-speed sleigh ride. When the dust settled, he was helped from the cockpit by the Mobile Control crew for that day, Willie Lawson and Gil Martinez. Despite four 9th SRW aircraft losses between 13 April 1967 and 10 October 1968, Category III 'Operational' Testing continued until December 1968. The Wing was awarded the Presidential Unit Citation for meeting the challenges of bringing the 'most advanced' reconnaissance system of its day to a state of operational readiness.

On 17 June 1970 the 9th lost another SR-71A, serial '970, following a mid-air collision with a KC-135Q shortly after taking aboard 35,000 lb (15876 kg) of fuel. The SR-71 hit clear air turbulence (CAT) and the entire nose of the aircraft smashed into the rear of the tanker. No one aboard the tanker was injured and both Buddy Brown and Mort Jarvis were able to eject safely – although the former broke both legs during the ejection.

Frank Murray also captured this image of a North Korean airfield during his 1965 A-12 overflight. (National Archive via Tim Brown)

4. Operational History: SR-71 Operations from Kadena

Strategic Air Command was both a major command of the US Air Force and a Joint Chiefs of Staff (JCS) specified command. Headquarters USAF assigned SAC the responsibility for all strategic reconnaissance and the command executed its mission under the supervision and guidance of the Chief of Staff, US Air Force. In part, the Commander in Chief SAC (CINCSAC – pronounced 'sink sack') was directed, 'to prepare plans for strategic aerospace reconnaissance for which the Air Force [was] responsible (electronic, weather, visual, aerial, photographic, cartographic, reproduction, and related activities) to meet the global requirements of the Department of Defense'. As a specified command, SAC received assignments directly from the JCS, which included photographic and signal coverage of selected areas together with global upper atmospheric sampling. Requirements for individual reconnaissance programmes were specified and outlined in operations and fragmentary orders (orders coming from a higher level) and through its Strategic Reconnaissance Center (SRC), at Offutt AFB, Nebraska. Headquarters SAC exercised operational control over all such missions, supervising their planning, scheduling and execution, unless such functions had been specially delegated in a SAC operational order. In the specific case of SR-71 operations, codenamed Giant Elk by SAC, these were planned by specialists in the SR-71 branch at the SRC in response to tasking by the JCS, initially in support of the SAC Single Integrated Operational Plan (SIOP), the Defense Intelligence

Agency (DIA), the Commander in Chief Pacific (CINCPAC), Seventh Air Force, Military Assistance Command Vietnam and Commander United States Air Forces in Korea (COMUSKOREA). Senior Officers at the SRC took part in two daily meetings, one held at 7:30 a.m., the other at 3:30 p.m., to review current mission tasking, planning and the weather. Once the SRC had completed the mission planning process, details were forwarded to the JCS for final approval.

OL-8

As the 9th SRW neared operational readiness, the decision was made by Col Bill Hayes (9th SRW Commander) and Col Hal Confer (Director of Operations) as to which crews would be first to be deployed to Kadena AB. Eight were selected and began training for the deployment, flying simulator sorties depicting the oceanic route they would fly. It was also decided that the same sequence of crew deployment to Kadena would be repeated, when it became time to fly operational missions over Vietnam. Initially, three aircraft and four crews would be deployed and the crews themselves pulled straws to decide the 'batting order'; the fourth crew would act as standby for the three deploying aircraft and would arrive on Kadena if their services were not needed, by KC-135Q tanker. Command of the operating location (OL-8) would alternate between the 9th SRW's wing commander and vice commander (and later Deputy Chief of Operations). The 'OL's' numbered designation was arrived at sequentially, after the 9th SRW's

With the underside panels of the nose section removed, the antenna for the Loral CAPRE high resolution, ground-mapping radar is revealed. Also visible, on the leading edge of the left wing to fuselage chine, are wedge-shaped areas of radar-absorbent material. (Lockheed)

U-2 detachments. Two days before Glowing Heat, a codename reserved for SR-71 positioning flights, six tankers were flown to Hickam AFB, Hawaii. Air refuelling support for the SR-71 was

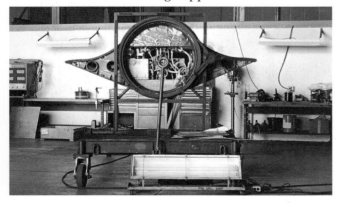

provided by SAC KC-135Q tankers, and was codenamed Giant Bear. Initially three units were designated to perform this vital task, the 903rd Air Refuelling Squadron (ARS) at Beale, the 306th ARS at McCoy and the 909th ARS at Kadena (on 1 July 1971 support was increased to four squadrons; the 9th and 903rd ARSs at Beale, the 306th ARS at McCoy and the 70th ARS at Little Rock). Emergency radio coverage was set up on Wake Island and all was ready for the first operational deployment.

On 8 March 1968, Major Buddy Brown and his RSO Dave Jenson left Beale in '978 and became

Its detachable nose section bestowed great versatility upon the SR-71A. Here the unit is mounted on its special dolly and houses a Loral CAPRE antenna assembly. (Paul F. Crickmore)

the first Senior Crown crew to deploy to Kadena. The flight involved three air refuellings and Buddy recalls, 'We had taken off from Beale at 11:00 and had arrived at Kadena at 09:05 – nearly two hours earlier than take off time (but in the next day because we had crossed the international date line). We beat the sun by a good margin.' Two days later Maj. Jerry O'Malley and Capt. Ed Payne delivered '976 to the OL and were followed on 13 March, by Bob Spencer and Keith Branham in '974. Finally, three days later, in late evening rain, Jim Watkins and Dave Dempster, the back-up crew, were wearily disgorged from a KC-135 Stratotanker, the crews and their mounts were ready for business.

Giant Scale

All missions flown against North Vietnam, Laos, Cambodia and North Korea were codenamed Giant Scale. Due to maintenance problems, Buddy Brown and Dave Jenson missed their chance of being the first crew to fly such a sortie; instead, that accolade went to Maj. Jerry O'Malley and Capt. Ed Payne in '976. The historic mission was flown by them on Thursday 21 March 1968 and followed a route similar to that flown by Mele Vojvodich in his A-12, ten months earlier. However, configured with both cameras and a Goodyear Side-Looking Airborne Radar (SLAR), located in its detachable nose section, the SR-71 promised to deliver much more comprehensive coverage of that same 'collection area'.

Having refuelled after the first run over Thailand, Jerry climbed and accelerated on track for their final 'take' of the mission, which was to pass over the DMZ. For this, the primary sensor was the SLAR. On arrival back at Kadena Jerry and Ed were confronted with a base completely 'fogged in'. Despite a good Ground Controlled Approach (GCA), Jerry never saw the runway and climbed back to contemplate further options. With the SR low on fuel, another tanker was launched and 25,000 lb (11340 kg) of additional fuel was taken onboard. The crew then received a two-figure encoded number that told them to divert to Taiwan. So, in company with two tankers and with the SR-71 adopting a tanker callsign for security reasons, the three-ship formation made its slow, lumbering way to Ching Chuan Kang (CCK). On arrival the SR-71 was quickly hangared and the next day the 'take' was downloaded and despatched for processing; the film to the 67th RTS at Yokota AB, Japan and the SLAR imagery to the 9th RTS at Beale AFB. After two nights at CCK, Jerry and Ed ferried '976 back to Kadena and were greeted by a superb reception from their friends.

Post-mission intelligence results were stunning. The SLAR imagery revealed the location of many artillery emplacements around Khe Sanh, and a huge truck park that was used to support the guns; these sites had eluded US sensors on other recce aircraft up to that point. Over the next few days, air strikes were mounted against both targets, reducing their effectiveness dramatically. After a 77-day siege, Khe Sanh was at last relieved on 7 April 1968

The 40-ft (12-m) diameter main brake 'chute provided a high level of deceleration during the landing roll-out. As with many fast jets, the SR-71 employed a brake 'chute both as a means to shorten its landing roll and to extend the life of its wheel brakes.(Paul F. Crickmore)

(two weeks after '976's discovery sortie). As a result of their highly successful mission both Maj. Jerome F. O'Malley and Capt. Edward D. Payne were awarded the Distinguished Flying Cross. On its debut operational mission, the Lockheed SR-71 had proved its value.

Early OL-8 operational sorties were typified by problems involving the SR-71's generators, this often led to the aircraft having to divert into one of the USAF bases in Thailand. Of the 168 SR-71 sorties flown by the detachment throughout 1968, some 67 were operational missions over North Vietnam, the remaining sorties being FCFs or for crew training. In addition the first of many aircraft redeployments took place when during a seven-day period in September, aircraft '980, '970 and '962 took over from '978, '976 and '974. Crew rotation took place every 30 days, with no less than 21 crews having taken the SR-71 into battle

over the same period. Also during this time, the SR-71 received its nickname 'Habu'. The Habu is a poisonous pit viper found on the Ryuku Islands: though non-aggressive, it can inflict a painful bite if provoked. Although resisted by officialdom, the name Habu has proved to be permanent among all associated with the Senior Crown programme.

OL-8 lost its first Habu after more than two years of Kadena operations, on 10 May 1970. Majors Willie Lawson and Gil Martinez had completed one pass over North Vietnam and had air refuelled '969 near Korat RTAFB (Royal Thai Air Force Base). Having initiated an

Right: With the high-speed boom lowered by the tanker, the SR-71 moves into the contact position. This is a formation task for the pilots, as it is down to the highly skilled boom operator to 'fly' the boom into the receiver's refuelling receptacle. (Paul F. Crickmore)

Groundcrews at Kadena used individual 'Habu' markings to record successful operational sorties. This set of 'Habus' belonged to 64-17974, the aircraft also carrying the name *Ichi Ban*. The Kadena-based detachment suffered some operational losses, but none attributable to enemy action. (Aerospace Publishing Ltd)

Three of the J58's six low-compression-ratio bypass ducts can clearly be seen in this view. The ducts feed bleed air from the fourth stage of the compressor into the turbine exhaust, enabling the engine to function over the SR-71's vast speed range. An engine problem on 27 September 1971 caused major headaches for Bob Spencer and Butch Sheffield during a particularly sensitive mission. (Pratt & Whitney)

afterburner climb prior to the 'dipsy doodle' manoeuvre, they discovered they were surrounded by heavy thunderclouds extending up to 50,000 ft (15240 m). Needing climb distance to get above the clouds before commencing the dip-manoeuvre, and with the aircraft sluggish with its full fuel load, Willie eased '969 into a slightly steeper climb, trying to clear a 30,000 ft (9144 m) saddleback of cloud. At that moment the aircraft entered turbulent cloud and both engines flamed out; the aircraft's angle of attack increased, then suddenly the nose pitched-up and recovery was impossible. Both crewmembers ejected safely and landed resplendent in their silver moon suits, near

U-Tapao RTAFB, Thailand. This was the fourth SR-71 Blackbird to be lost in a pitch-up incident.

Although the vast majority of early Habu flights from Kadena were Giant Scale sorties, this was not exclusively the case. On the night of 27 September 1971, Majors Bob Spencer and Butch Sheffield completed post-take-off tanking and established '980 on a northerly track. US Intelligence had obtained details of a large Soviet naval exercise to be held near Vladivostok, in the Sea of Japan; such an event could prove a rich fishing ground for an electromagnetic intelligence trawl, and the Habu was ideal for stirring up the Soviet fleet's defence systems.

National security officials were especially

interested in obtaining signal details relating to the Soviet's new SA-5 SAM system. Accordingly Major Jack Clemance, an innovative Electronic Warfare Officer who worked in the 9th SRW's Electronic Data Processing Centre, jury-rigged one of the aircraft's Elint sensors which allowed it to receive continuous-wave signal data.

As '980 bore down on the target area, dozens of Soviet radars were switched on, but just short of entering Soviet airspace the Habu rolled into a 35° banked turn, remaining throughout in international airspace. However, on approach to the target area, Bob noted the right engine's oil pressure was dipping. Clearing the area, he once again scanned the engine instruments only to discover that the needle had fallen to 'zero'. He shut down the engine and was forced to descend and decelerate to subsonic speeds. Having stirred up a hornets' nest, they were now sitting ducks for any Soviet fast jets sent up to intercept the oil-starved Habu. Worse still, at lower altitude they were subjected to strong headwinds that rapidly depleted their fuel supply. Butch calculated that recovery back to

Kadena was out of the question – instead they would have to divert into South Korea.

The OL commander had been monitoring '980's slow progress and as the Habu neared Korea, US listening posts reported the launch of several MiGs from Pyongyang, North Korea. In response, USAF Convair F-102 Delta Daggers were scrambled from a base near Hon Chew, South Korea and vectored into a position between the Habu and the MiGs. It was later established that the MiG launch was unconnected with the Habu's descent and Bob recovered '980 into Taegu, South Korea, without further incident. In all their EMR 'take' had recorded emissions from 290 different radars, but the greatest prize was the 'capture' of the first, and much sought-after SA-5 signals.

Bombing halt

The US bombing halt of North Vietnam came to an end on 30 March 1972, when the communist North began an all out invasion of South Vietnam. Five B-52 strikes were launched against key logistics targets between 9 and 23 April,

When all final ground checks have been completed, maintenance engineers await the signal from their Crew Chief to remove the wheel chocks, after which the aircraft is cleared by air traffic control to enter the runway, line up and hold. (Paul F. Crickmore)

SR-71/KC-135Q tanking operations were typically conducted at 350 kt (403 mph; 649 km/h) and 26,000 ft (7925 m); this envelope was some way from perfect for the Habu, but was about as high as a fully laden '135 could operate at 350 kt. (Paul F. Crickmore)

signalling the start of an operation codenamed Linebacker I. SAC was requested to increase the number of SR-71 reconnaissance sorties to obtain imagery for bomb damage assessment. On 8 May, as the war escalated, President Nixon ordered that routes into and out of North Vietnam harbours should be mined. The next day, in an operation codenamed Pocket Money, the JCS directed that drones and the SR-71 should photograph, on a daily basis, the ports of Haiphong, Hon Gai, Gam Pha, Dong Hoi, Quang Khe, Vinh and Thanh Hoa, to identify the enemy's shipping channels in readiness for US Navy mining operations. One week into the operation, the JCS designated the Loral High Resolution Radar (HRR), as an acceptable sensor for this purpose. This was the first occasion that the JCS had specifically directed that the HRR should cover a predetermined intelligence target and by so doing, they signalled that the

technology had officially come of age.

In June, the JCS required the SR-71 to photograph communication and logistics supply lines between the North Vietnamese ports and Chinese border areas. Throughout this time the SR-71 also used its sophisticated electromagnetic reconnaissance (EMR) system to collect Elint, as part of SAC's Combat Apple Sigint collection operation in Southeast Asia which also utilised the U-2 and RC-135. As the situation on the ground deteriorated, additional B-52s were deployed to the region and by late June the 200 giant eight-engined bombers deployed to the region were chalking up over 3,100 sorties per month. They were also having a decisive effect on the North's invasion.

On 20 July 1972, while returning to Kadena from an operational mission over North Vietnam, Majors Denny Bush and Jimmy Fagg were caught shortly after touch-down in '978, by

B-52 sorties were flown. Two chaff corridors were sown by F-4s in an attempt to protect the large bombers, but 100-kt (115-mph; 185-km/h) winds dispersed the metallic cloud before the BUFFs (big ugly fat f***ers) arrived. CHARCOAL 1, a B-52G leading nine other Guam-based aircraft against the Yen Vien/Ai Mo warehouse area, took hits from two SA-2s and became the first B-52 lost to hostile action during the war. Two other bombers also fell victim to some of the 164 SA-2s launched that night.

Day Two saw 93 B-52s striking targets that included the Radio Hanoi station, Yen Vien, Bac Giang, Kinh No and Thai Nguyen. Yet again, some 200 SA-2s were fired, but no aircraft were lost; however, on the night of 20 December six B-52s were downed and by Christmas Eve (Day Seven of the battle) 11 B-52s had been shot down. After a 36-hour pause over Christmas, operations resumed. Using revised tactics, 113 aircraft battered ten different targets in seven 15-minute waves. Two more B-52s were shot down by SA-2s despite the strike force being supported by more than 100 fighter-bombers that were used to suppress SAM batteries in the Haiphong area.

An hour before midnight on 27 December 1972, Giant Scale mission GS663 got underway, when SR-71 '975 lifted off Kadena's runway on what would prove to be the only Habu night sortie of the entire Vietnam War. Col Darrell Cobb and RSO, Capt. Reggie Blackwell's mission objective was to conduct a coordinated EMR/HRR sortie, to determine if the North Vietnamese had acquired new equipment or employed updated procedures for the SA-2s that were responsible for achieving such high B-52 losses. To achieve this, their arrival over the Haiphong–Hanoi areas was timed at precisely the same moment that 60 B-52s were to begin dropping their bombs on the rail yards at Lang Dang, Duc Noi and Trung Quant, the Van Dien supply centre and three missile sites. With the North's defensive radar systems running at full stretch to cope with the raid, intelligence planners reasoned that this would be an ideal time for such a sortie. In addition, the SR-71 with its unmatched ECM suite would provide additional electronic support for the bombers.

As the SR-71 arrived over the collection area, bang on schedule, the crew observed numerous

excessive cross-winds. Jettisoning the 'chute as per the book to prevent the aircraft from 'weather-cocking' sharply into wind, the extended rollout caused the aircraft to roll off the end of the runway, and in a twist of fate it hit the concrete housing of the emergency crash barriers. One of the main landing gear struts was badly damaged which in turn caused substantial additional damage. Both crewmembers were unhurt, but '978 was written off.

In late October 1972, President Nixon called a halt to bombing north of the 20th Parallel in anticipation of a truce. But as a hedge against the talks becoming deadlocked or breaking up, he ordered the JCS to draw up contingency plans that would concentrate overwhelming fire power on the areas of Hanoi–Haiphong. On 13 December 1972, the North Vietnamese delegation walked out of the Paris Peace Talks and two days later Nixon authorised the unleashing of Linebacker II. Initially planned as a three-day campaign, it was extended to an eleven-day all-out night offensive by the B-52s. Day One began on 18 December 1972, when 129

Before any sortie, the Crew Chief directed the aircraft to a halt and maintenance specialists chocked the wheels prior to further external checks. To obtain maximum engine efficiency, the pilot then fine-tuned the engine exhaust gas temperature (EGT), before engaging the engine trim. (Paul F. Crickmore)

SA-2 firings and while transiting, they were able to radiate a blinding ECM blanket with their advanced defensive systems that no doubt contributed to reducing the B-52 loss-rate of this raid to two aircraft. The crew of '975 landed back at the detachment at 02:39 in the morning; subsequent analysis of their Elint data revealed a wealth of information, including the discovery of two emitters that had been responsible for heavy B-52 losses. The two 60-bomber raids launched on the final two nights of Linebacker II saw all B-52s arrive back at their bases safely. Following the action on the night of 29/30 December, the North Vietnamese government expressed a willingness to return to the negotiating table. President Nixon ordered a halt to the attacks and on 27 January 1973, Le Duc Tho, the North Vietnamese foreign minister, and Henry Kissinger signed the Peace Accord in Paris that spelled an end to US armed forces involvement in Vietnam.

Giant Scale II

In May 1978, Vietnam began a series of border skirmishes with Kampuchea and in late December these escalated into a full-scale invasion. Following the fall of Phnom Penh on

7 January 1979, the Vietnamese-backed rebel forces declared Pol Pot and the infamous Khmer Rouge to be overthrown and formed a government. However, fighting between the rival factions continued in the west of the country, creating in the process thousands of refugees who fled into neighbouring Thailand. Concerned that an estimated army of 200,000 Vietnamese regulars in Kampuchea might turn their weapons on them, the Thai government requested reconnaissance coverage of the area from its long standing ally, the United States. In total, five SR-71 sorties were flown in support of this request, the first by Tom Keck and Tim Shaw in serial '979 on 17 February 1980. This was followed by Rick Young and Russ Szcepanik, again in '979, on 3 May; Gil Bertelson and Frank Stampf completed a 6 hour 12 minute sortie in '976 on 3 August: Bob Crowder and John Morgan chalked up their mission in '960 on 22 November and BC Thomas and Jay Reid completed the series of sorties codenamed Giant Scale II by SAC, in '976 on 24 November. Each round robin (return) sortie from Kadena covered approximately 6,500 miles (10461 km) and required three air refuellings; one over the Philippine Sea and the other two over the Gulf of

After receiving take-off clearance from the air traffic control tower – sometimes this was in the form of a single green light to enhance RT (radio) security – the pilot eased both throttles into the mid-afterburner position, this causing a slight left/right yaw as first one then the other burner kicked in. (Paul F. Crickmore)

A tradition with one particular pilot on completion of an operational sortie was to fly fast and at extremely low level down the main runway. In general, the SR was not a particularly happy bird at low level, but nevertheless gave some stunning air show performances, most notably at RAF Mildenhall's annual Air Fete. Indeed, such was the show put on by Major Jim Jiggins in '973 at the 1987 Air Fete, that the aircraft was overstressed and had to be retired. (Paul F. Crickmore)

Thailand. All five were photographic intelligence (Photint) missions with the aircraft configured with an Optical Bar Camera (OBC) unit in the nose and Technical Objective Cameras (TEOCs) in the chine bays. Four of the five sorties secured standard black and white imagery of the target area, however the JCS directed that the cameras for the mission flown in '960 should be loaded with Kodak SO-131 camouflage detection film. This film coloured healthy vegetation red and dead or dying vegetation various shades of grey and white. This was used to gauge the probable yield of Kampuchea's rice crop. The country had become a member of the United Nations in September 1980 and, after processing, the imagery was forwarded to the DIA where it helped the US to plan its contribution level to the UN food relief programme for Kampuchea. The rest of the reconnaissance imagery collected during the other four sorties failed to reveal any large concentrations of Vietnamese forces or equipment along the Thai border and after

sanitising the photography, it was passed, via the US Embassy in Bangkok, to high-level officials in the Thai government.

Giant Cobra and Giant Express

The Horn of Africa is an immensely important strategic location, 'guarding' the Red Sea approach to the Suez Canal and overlooking the 'oil arteries' of Saudi Arabia, Iraq, Oman, Kuwait, Djibouti and the United Arab Emirates as they fan out from the southern entrance to the Red Sea. In August 1977 a war broke out between communist-governed Ethiopia and its neighbour, Somalia. In November that same year, the Soviet Union began airlifting arms to Ethiopia and these were backed-up by Cuban troops, sent by Fidel Castro. By March 1978, it was estimated that approximately 11,000 Cuban troops were 'in-country', and two Soviet generals were directing the ground war against Somalia. Accordingly, the JCS directed that SAC should position a Kadena-based SR-71 to Diego

The SR-71 used a drogue chute to remove a cover from the main brake parachute system. In this case the aircraft is SR-71B serial '956. Note the ventral fins under each engine nacelle – these were installed to improve longitudinal stability, which was compromised by the raised second cockpit. (Paul F. Crickmore)

Garcia, a small British-owned island in the Indian Ocean, and plan a round-robin Photint reconnaissance mission over the area to monitor the extent of Soviet and Cuban presence. In response, the SRC prepared a track for such a sortie and the JCS directed that the flight should launch on 12 March 1978; however, the theatre situation changed dramatically earlier in the month when Somalia suddenly withdrew its troops from Ethiopia and agreed to keep them out, provided that all foreign troops consented to leave the region. As a result, the mission was cancelled even before the SR-71 had been positioned on the tiny island. The event however, proved to be a catalyst in preparing Diego Garcia to support SR-71 contingency operations in the Indian Ocean area. In just three weeks from mid-February, an SR-71 shelter at Beale had been dismantled, transported to, and re-erected on, Diego Garcia, where a water

The last SR-71 to have been lost in an accident was aircraft '974, which crashed into the Pacific on 21 April 1989. The image below shows the remains of the cockpit. Both the pilot Maj. Dan House and his RSO Capt. Blair Bozek ejected safely. (Paul F. Crickmore collection)

Aircraft '968 was photographed as it cleared a tanker. For a time this aircraft remained on USAF strength, albeit in storage at Palmdale's Site 2, but was not one of those temporarily returned to duty in 1995. It now resides at the Richmond Air Museum in Virginia. (Lockheed Martin Skunk Works)

demineralisation plant, rations and a number of 376th Strategic Wing, KC-135Qs with JP-7 fuel were also positioned. The fragmentary order for any such contingency operations in this theatre was initially codenamed Giant Cobra.

As the region slipped into further political upheaval, with the rise to power of Ayatollah Khomeini and his brand of Islamic fundamentalism in Iran, and Soviet involvement in Afghanistan, it was decided to further bolster facilities on Diego Garcia, in the event that the national intelligence users required more extensive coverage of the area. On 2 April 1979, the JCS directed SAC to create a permanent SR-71 fuel storage facility on Diego Garcia. Initially, two 50,000-US gal (189265-litre) polyurethane fuel storage bladders were

deployed and filled by ten Kadena-based KC-135Qs in an operation codenamed Giant Ace. On 1 May 1979, a follow-on fragmentary order, codenamed Giant Express, took cognisance of the deteriorating situation and included not only the Indian Ocean area, but also Africa and Southwest Asia as potential theatres of operation from Diego Garcia. Further developments on the island, by the US Navy, eventually freed-up a 1.26 million-US gallon (4.78 million-litre) fuel tank for prospective SR-71 operations. This was filled with JP-7 delivered by an ocean tanker. During the summer of 1980, the JCS approved a plan to exercise the newly created SR-71 facilities; consequently on 1 July, Bob Crowder and Don Emmons completed the 4 hour 24 minute flight to the island in '962. The flight

included three air refuellings, two from KC-135s operating from Kadena and a third from tankers that had been deployed a week earlier to Diego Garcia. The aircraft and crew returned to Kadena on 4 July, but despite validating the facilities and subsequent sorties being flown in the region, SR-71s never returned to the tropical island.

North Korea

As referred to earlier, the CIA-operated A-12 Oxcart programme conducted two overflights of North Korea, before early retirement led to the Senior Crown programme inheriting its missions. These were conducted from Kadena, with most of the operational objectives being achieved from international airspace, by flying either off the North Korean coast or over the de-militarised zone (DMZ).

In 1977, North Korea had an army of 450,000 men, but by mid 1978, the DIA and CIA believed that this had grown to between 550,000 and 600,000. The country's unpredictable dictator, Kim Il-sung, was committed to reunification of the peninsula under his form of communism, so in response to the increase in tension, a request was made by Admiral Maurice Weisner, (CINCPAC), to the JCS, who directed SAC to increase the number of monthly SR-71 monitoring sorties to the area from eight to twelve per month. The SRC then scheduled the SR-71 to be configured with cameras on two of the sorties and to gather Radar Intelligence (Radint) – using its HRR, and Elint sensors, on the remaining ten missions. The Photint provided a reference base for intel specialists to use when interpreting the HRR imagery.

North Korea's propensity to re-locate or reinforce its military units and installations along the DMZ at night prompted further requests from US theatre commanders that the majority of these SR-71 'indication and warning' sorties be conducted at night. This was communicated by the JCS to the SRC, and at 21:05, on 19 September 1977, Jack Veth and his RSO Bill Keller left Kadena in '960, returning 4 hours 6 minutes later, having completed the first night monitoring sortie of North Korea. The crews that flew these important missions were, however, less than impressed by their nocturnal forays, noting that the aircraft's cockpit lighting was uneven, causing reflections that made monitoring instrumentation extremely difficult and potentially dangerous, especially if the situation was further complicated by a lack of horizon; such conditions could well trigger vertigo and pilot disorientation, leading to the loss of an aircraft. To help alleviate the problem, the missions were flown at Mach 2.8 and with maximum bank angles of 35°. The situation was finally rectified in 1982, after the cockpit lighting had been improved and Peripheral Vision Horizon Display (PVHD) units were fitted in the SR-71 fleet. These units projected a thin red line of light across the aircraft's instrument panel to produce an artificial horizon that responded to changes in pitch and roll, thereby duplicating the behaviour of a natural horizon.

In April 1981, U-2R and SR-71 sorties began collecting Elint cuts and other raw data on a suspected SA-2 site that was under construction on the island of Choc Tarrie, in an estuary near the western end of Korea's DMZ. Throughout August the site was monitored closely as it became increasingly apparent that the North Koreans were about to embark upon another belligerent adventure.

At 10:00, on 25 August, Majors Nevin Cunningham and Geno Quist climbed into '967 for a two-loop sortie of the DMZ, or 'Z' as it was referred to by the SR-71 crew force. With the SR configured for an HRR and Elint sortie, the weather clear, and with fuel to spare, Nevin flicked the fuel dump switch during the final pass and in a quick Morse-code burst, spelled out a four letter expletive for the benefit of the North Korean ground trackers who were attempting to follow the SR-71 visually. Their humour was probably lost on the enemy, but it caused a few laughs back at the Habu bar at the Kadena base.

The next morning, Maj. Maury Rosenberg and RSO Capt. ED McKim were briefed for their mission, this entailed three passes along the DMZ. It was during the course of their third pass while flying from east to west in '976 at Mach 3 and 77,000 ft (23470 m), that ED remarked that he was getting DEF activity and that everything was turned on. In the next breath he exclaimed, 'Wow! It looks like we've had a launch'. Maury increased speed to Mach 3.2 and located the SA-2 missile's contrail, after which he made a turn to the left, taking them further away from the missile and deeper into South Korean airspace, from where he was able to watch the missile explode a good 2 miles (3 km) away.

The incident was of such importance that a coded message was despatched to all interested agencies including the National Security Council. Secretary of Defense Caspar Weinberger informed President Reagan who was said to be 'furious' over the incident; but while diplomatic exchanges between North Korea and the United States continued, the Korean monitoring sorties resumed, with the SR-71's reconnaissance track moved even further south. Then, on 26 October 1981, BC Thomas and Jay Reid left Kadena, in '975, on a flight that replicated that flown earlier by '976. This time Wild Weasel anti-radar strike aircraft were airborne and on hand. Should the North Koreans choose to launch another SA-2 at the SR-71 'decoy', the SAM site would have been taken out within 60 seconds of the launch. It was a plan that had been personally approved by the president himself, but, perhaps luckily for all involved, the North Koreans did not respond and the aircraft recovered safely back at Kadena 4 hours and 12 minutes later.

The last Habu loss during USAF ops occurred on 21 April 1989. On that occasion one of the engine compressor discs disintegrated during Mach 3 flight, the debris severing one hydraulic system and damaging the other. Lt Col Dan House and RSO Maj. Blair Bozek had decelerated and descended '974 down to 400 kt (460 mph; 740 km/h) and 10,000 ft (3048 m) when the remaining hydraulic system ran dry. Both men safely ejected just a few hundred yards off the coast of Luzon and were rescued by Filipino fishermen. They were later picked up by an HH-53 helicopter and flown to Clark AFB.

OL-8 was re-designated OL RK on 30 October 1970, and became OL KA on 26 October 1971; finally being designated Detachment 1, or Det 1, of the 9th SRW in August 1974, a title it retained until deactivated in 1990. During 22 years of service, the unit flew missions to Vietnam, Laos, Cambodia, Thailand, North Korea and in airspace off the USSR and China, and completed four 11-hour return flights to the Persian Gulf during the Iran-Iraq war, underlining the importance of manned strategic reconnaissance as a means of both gathering intelligence and projecting power anywhere around the globe.

This shot of aircraft '958 travelling at less than Mach 1.6 illustrates nicely the fully forward position of the inlet spikes. Also shown to advantage are the open bypass doors in the forward section of the starboard engine nacelle. (Lockheed Martin Skunk Works)

5. Operational History: Beale and Det 4 Operations

Giant Reach was SAC's codename for the contingency planning of Europe-based SR-71 Photint and Elint gathering operations. Coverage was split, to include both photo reconnaissance and Elint of the Middle East, and purely Elint of Eastern Europe. These preliminary proposals, first published by HQ SAC on 6 April 1970, envisaged five KC-135Qs being deployed to Incirlik AB, Turkey, plus an SR-71 together with three KC-135s, and support personnel being assigned to RAF Mildenhall, Suffolk, England, on a 30-day, temporary duty (TDY) basis. Ideally, SAC would have preferred to base the SR-71 element of the operation at Torrejon AB, Spain; however, the Spanish prohibited overt reconnaissance flights from originating from their country. During these European deployments it was envisaged that between six and eight sorties would be flown; the photo product was to be processed by the 497th RTG (Reconnaissance Technical Group), at Schierstein ADM, West Germany and the Elint take analysed by the 9th RTS, at Beale. Additional funds to support such operations were not initially available; but HQ USAF directed SAC to spend $50,000 from its Operation and Maintenance budget on an apron adjacent to Hangar 538, at Mildenhall, in the event that the JCS should direct that such sorties should go ahead, and this construction work was completed in 1971.

At 14:00 (Local), on 6 October 1973 (Yom Kippur – the Jewish Day of Atonement), the State of Israel was bombed from the air and pounded by a massive artillery barrage from Egyptian and Syrian forces. This was swiftly followed by an invasion of Syrian troops to the north and a thrust by the Egyptian Army into the Sinai, from the west.

Yom Kippur

At war's outbreak, the only reconnaissance gathering satellites in orbit and available to the United States intelligence community were one KH-8 and one KH-9. To provide the decision makers in Washington with the most up-to-date battlefield intelligence, a rapid deployment of other recce assets into the region was essential. However, the sophisticated nature of the ground-to-air threat meant that only the SR-71 was capable of carrying out survivable, simultaneous synoptic (Photint and Elint) coverage of this 'denied area'. Consequently, CINCSAC General John Meyer, ordered Col Pat Halloran (9th SRW Commander) to prepare for missions that would be flown from Beale, across the war zone, and recover into RAF Mildenhall. With plans in place, Pat climbed aboard a KC-135 and departed for the large Suffolk base on 10 October. Upon arrival, he was immediately informed that clearance for such missions would not be granted. The UK's Heath government had turned its back on an historic ally in what would soon prove to be a futile attempt aimed at securing the continued supply of Arab oil. The KC-135 was then fuelled up and flown back to the US; undoubtedly the shortest overseas TDY in the history of the 9th SRW! The only alternative option to secure the required reconnaissance information was to plan a series

Aircraft '964 was nicknamed *The Bodonian Express* after it was forced to divert into Bodo in Norway with a technical fault on a mission from Beale. It is seen above with its name on the fin and at right taking the first half of a split load from a KC-135Q Stratotanker. (Paul F. Crickmore collection)

of round-robin missions flown from Griffiss AFB, New York. Additional ground support would be provided by Palmdale's flight test team which was already at the east coast base, conducting a series of evaluations with SR-71A '955, on a new A-2 electronic defence system; conveniently, the evaluation also provided security cover for the reconnaissance operation.

Accordingly, at 22:00 on 11 October 1973, Lt Col Jim Shelton and Maj. Gary Coleman left Beale in '979 and headed for Griffiss. On arrival they were met by an angry base commander and three Lockheed tech reps after laying 'a heavy late night sonic boom track' down into New York State as they descended from altitude. A telephone call from Jim to Al Joernz and John Fuller (who would fly a second SR-71 into Griffiss) advised them to move their descent profile over the Great Lakes to minimise the effects of the boom on urban eastern states. With the amendment incorporated into their flight plan no boom complaints accompanied the arrival of '964. Unfortunately this second aircraft developed a hydraulic problem that forced an engine change, leaving the new detachment down to one mission-ready aircraft until

specialised equipment could be flown in from Beale. An hour after the arrival of '964, the first tanker from Beale touched down carrying Tom Estes (the Operations Officer), three mission planners and a number of the 9th's best intelligence and maintenance personnel. At 06:00 a secure teleprinter clattered out details of the first sortie that was to be flown 22 hours later.

When the crews met the mission planners the former voiced concerns about a lack of diversionary fields, but no one could offer a satisfactory answer. Later that morning, a tanker from Mildenhall arrived and technicians began preparing '979 for the longest operational sortie to date. By mid-afternoon it was suggested that the crew should get some sleep since they had been up nearly 36 hours and would soon be readying themselves for a 16-hour day. They were directed to old quarters where they discovered their rooms to be hot and their beds uncomfortable. Gary Coleman recalled, 'No one could snore like Jim Shelton and I got no sleep at all, but I consoled myself with the thought that at least my pilot was getting some solid rest!'

The belligerent attitude of usually helpful allies required JP-7 fuel and tanker crews to be repositioned from Mildenhall and Incirlik, to Zaragoza in Spain and the quest for emergency landing sites was proving all but impossible. Nevertheless, Jim Shelton cranked '979's engines on cue and lifted off from Griffiss at 02:00, on the first of nine Giant Reach/Busy Pilot missions. He made good the first of six aerial refuellings (there were two tankers in each AR track), off the Gulf of St Lawrence (a point known to the crews as Old Barge East). Having topped-off, '979 then accelerated and climbed east, en route to the next cell of tankers awaiting the thirsty Habu off the coast of Portugal (Rota East). Returning again to speed and altitude, it made a high-Mach dash through the Straits of Gibraltar and let-down for a third AR, south of Crete (Crete East). Due to

When the SR-71 was based in Europe, opportunities for formation photographs sometimes arose. Here aircraft '980 flies with a No. 41 Squadron, RAF, Jaguar GR.Mk 1 – a somewhat lower-performing tactical reconnaissance asset – from RAF Coltishall in the spring of 1982. (Crown Copyright)

the Habu's proximity to the war zone and Libya, the US Navy provided a CAP (Combat Air Patrol), from carrier based aircraft on station in the Mediterranean.

Shelton and Coleman then resumed their climb and acceleration to coast-in over Port Said. Gary Coleman comments, 'There was no indication of anything launched against us, but everyone was painting us on their radars as we made our turn inbound. The DEF panel lit up like a pin-ball machine and I said to Jim, "This should be interesting." In all, '979 spent 25 minutes over 'denied territory'. Entering Egyptian airspace at 11:03 GMT, it covered the Israeli battle fronts with both Egypt and Syria before coasting out and letting down for its fourth Air Refuelling Control Point (ARCP) (Crete West), which was still being CAPed by the US Navy.

Its next hot leg was punctuated by a fifth refuelling, again off Portugal (Rota West), before a final high-speed run across the western Atlantic towards New York. Mindful of his own fatigue, Gary was in awe of his pilot who completed a text-book sixth air refuelling (Old Barge West), before greasing '979 back down at Griffiss after a combat sortie lasting ten hours 18 minutes (more than 5 hours of which was at Mach 3 or above) and involving support from fourteen ever dependable KC-135Qs, four from the Canadian base at Goose Bay, two from

Griffiss and eight from Torrejon. The reconnaissance 'take' was of 'high quality' and provided intelligence and defence analysts with much needed information concerning the disposition of Arab forces (and Soviet equipment), in the region, which was then made available to the Israelis.

Aircraft '979 paid a second successful visit to the Yom Kippur war zone on 25 October; due to protestations from the Spanish government, the second and fifth AR tracks were re-positioned off the coast of the Azores and renamed Lajes East and Lajes West. As the US intelligence community was concerned that the Soviet Union might deploy personnel and material to the Arabs, the mission's priority objectives were to monitor port facilities at Latakia and Tartus in Syria and Port Said and Alexandria in Egypt. A third mission was chalked-up by the same aircraft eight days later. In addition to photography of the ports, national intelligence users also requested coverage of Cairo International airport and the Tura cave facilities also near Cairo, which it was believed might contain Soviet 'Scud-B' mobile missiles. Majors Jim Wilson and Bruce Douglas took '964 on its first sortie to the Mediterranean on 11 November. The 10-hour 45-minute flight departed Griffiss and terminated as planned at Seymour Johnson AFB, North Carolina. The

Aircraft '972 lands back at Mildenhall after an operational flight. Note the lack of any national markings which is technically against the Hague Convention of 1907 that states that all military aircraft must bear conspicuously placed insignia. (Paul F. Crickmore)

In terms of aircraft numbers, SR operations were always a minor part of RAF Mildenhall's duties. By far the majority of the base's resources were aimed at supporting transport and tanking operations, although EC-135 command posts were based there and 'the Hall' is no stranger to RC-135 Elint aircraft. (Paul F. Crickmore)

reason behind this detachment migration to the south was to avoid New York's winter weather.

Despite hostilities between the factions officially ending with a Soviet-backed motion in the United Nations on 24 October, fierce fire-fighting continued to flare up at regular intervals and it was to cover the disengagement and withdrawal of opposing armies that the SR-71's monitoring system continued to be called upon, with five further marathon flights being flown from Seymour Johnson.

Planning for records

The series of long-range Middle East missions represents a pinnacle of operational professionalism and serves as a tribute, not only to the dedication of the aircrews, but also to that of the staff planners, KC-135 tanker crews and of course the unsung heroes, that small group of top ground technicians who maintained the SR-71s away from home. The sorties also stand as a testament to the long reach capability of the aircraft and its ability to operate, on short notice, with little risk of interception in a very high-threat environment.

As part of the United States bicentennial celebrations SAC and HQ USAF agreed to reveal some of the SR-71's performance capabilities, by securing for the nation more records. Initially the

plan was to set an 'around the world at the equator' speed record. Pat Bledsoe and John Fuller were the senior crew at the time and were chosen to make the flight. Initial planning showed it could be done in 16 hours 20 minutes with fuel taken onboard from seven air refuelling tracks. The only modification for the SR-71 would have been an additional liquid nitrogen dewar for fuel tank pressurisation. Alas though, the planning came to an abrupt halt when Air Force generals saw the cost of deploying fuel and tankers to forward bases around the world – it would involve almost 100 KC-135 flights! Instead a new set of world speed and altitude records was set by the 9th, on 27 and 28 July 1976.

Cuba

Early in the Senior Crown Programme, Cuban reconnaissance sorties became a task covered by SR-71s of the 9th SRW. Flown from Beale and initially codenamed Giant Plate, they were subsequently renamed as Clipper. Most sorties were 'stand-off' runs, flown abeam the island in international airspace. Such missions would typically take 3 hours 30 minutes to complete and were considered very routine.

Occasionally however, the track was modified to take the aircraft directly over Cuba. When the

A Blackbird take-off is always a spectacular event. Once airborne the aircraft builds up speed rapidly, but is restricted from the rocket-like acceleration that might be expected by its relatively low *g* limits. (Paul F. Crickmore)

Carter administration entered office, it suspended all overflight activity in an act of 'goodwill'. In 1978 however, a reconnaissance satellite photographed a Soviet freighter in Havana harbour surrounded by large crates that were being moved to a nearby air base where aircraft were being reassembled. It appeared that 15 MiG-23s had been supplied to the Cuban leader Castro's air force. The MiG-23BN 'Flogger-H' was known to be capable of carrying nuclear weapons and if it was this variant that had been exported, then the shipment violated the 1962 Soviet pledge of not deploying 'offensive' weapons to Cuba. Two SR-71 sorties were flown over Cuba in November 1978, verifying that the aircraft were MiG-23M 'Flogger-E's, optimised for air defence and substantiating the Soviet claims.

Losing support

Early in the Senior Crown programme, the total number of SR-71s funded to conduct operations was scaled down. The two flying squadrons became one in April 1971 and following US disengagement from Vietnam together with the end of the Yom Kippur War, the number of Primary Authorised Aircraft (PAA) – the number

of operational machines the unit was allowed to have on strength – also declined. By 1977, the number of PAAs stood at just six A models and the two-seat trainer; funding was therefore reduced proportionately.

The programme took a further knock from the powerful National Intelligence Committee, which had become seduced by 'the panacea' of satellite-generated intelligence products; this had the effect of further eroding SR-71 support. Headquarters USAF viewed the programme as a budget burden, tasked as it was by national agencies to support a variety of theatre intelligence requirements. HQ SAC was hostile because the SR diverted funds away from its bomber and tanker mission and although its Single Integrated Operational Plan (SIOP), for a full-on east-west war, required regular Sigint data to keep it current; the SR-71, unlike the RC-135 and U-2R, was not capable of gathering 'long-on-station' samples of Sigint, therefore loss of its SAC patronage left the programme isolated and vulnerable to further budget cuts. To survive, the SR-71 had to compete with overhead (satellite) systems; but this required a major sensor upgrade that included an air-to-ground data link.

To provide the required 'near-real-time capability', a high level of investment was necessary, and it was thought that a new mission might provide the SR community with greater lobbying power, which in turn might provide the necessary leverage to appropriate funds required for the sensor upgrade. Therefore, in the mid-seventies a 'marketing package' was prepared by Pentagon-based Senior Crown advocates, which included details of the SR-71's performance and intelligence-gathering capabilities; the group then embarked on a public relations campaign within the Washington intelligence community to gather support for what appeared to be a mortally wounded programme.

An early port of call was a briefing to intelligence officers of the Navy's Atlantic fleet, where Bill Flexenhar (an analyst at the Naval Intelligence Support Centre at Suitland, Maryland), expressed an interest in the SR-71's sea-scanning radar capabilities to detect Soviet submarines. Of particular concern to Flexenhar was the Soviet Union's Northern fleet, which was headquartered at Severomorsk, located on the Kola Peninsula. Equipped with over a hundred nuclear-powered submarines, it was the biggest of three fleets and operated from ice-free, year-round berths, into the Barents and Norwegian Seas. From there, the submarines were capable of hitting targets in the United States, with their 4,800-mile (7725-km) range Submarine-Launched Ballistic Missiles (SLBMs). The region had proved to be particularly difficult to monitor via satellites due to cloud cover, so Flexenhar requested that those areas be 'SLAR-imaged' for his analysis. As a result, in May 1978 Admiral James L. Holloway III, Chief of Naval Operations requested the DIA to validate the requirement to utilise the SR-71 for such operations over those areas. This was denied however, on the basis of Senior Crown's commitments in other parts of the world. Instead two missions were flown over the Soviet's Pacific fleet near Vladivostok to collected Radint and test out the concept.

Mildenhall operations

As noted earlier, the first planned visit of an SR-71 to England was to have been on 11 October 1973, during the Yom Kippur War. In the event, it was not until 1 September 1974 that the UK received its first Habu, when a new transatlantic speed record of less than two hours was established. Eighteen months later, on 20 April 1976, the same aircraft – '972, returned for a ten-day deployment, using the callsign BURNS 31; however, on this occasion the 'visit'

was at the behest of the JCS; the mission objective being to monitor the twice-yearly Soviet/Warsaw Pact troop rotation.

Aircraft '962 was next to arrive at Mildenhall, during Exercise Teamwork on 6 September 1976; it stayed nineteen days, this time monitoring the autumn troop rotations – ensuring that the number of divisions deployed to Warsaw Pact countries during the spring tallied with the number of units withdrawn in the autumn.

On 7 January 1977, '958 arrived as RING 21; it left ten days later as PAVER 86; returning yet again on 16 May as INDY 69 to monitor the spring cycle of troop rotations, before flying back to Beale 15 days later as RESAY 35. These routine troop-monitoring missions continued with aircraft '976 covering the autumn of 1977 rotation between 24 October and 16 November, and '964 monitoring both the spring and autumn situation in 1978, from 24 April to 12 May and 16 October to 2 November. This routine was interrupted by the JCS however, when it directed that a special Photint mission should be flown.

Yemen

During the early spring of 1979, tensions between Saudi Arabia and the People's Republic of Yemen were strained to a point where the US intelligence community believed that the Republic was on the brink of invading its northern neighbour. As a result, on the morning of Monday 12 March, Majors Rich Graham and Don Emmons deployed '972 from Beale to Mildenhall in order to furnish decision makers with the necessary intelligence information. Following two early-morning ground aborts due to cloud cover over the 'collection area', a mission was finally launched; Buzz Carpenter and his RSO, John Murphy, got airborne and headed for their ARCP off Land's End. Unfortunately, Buzz suffered a violent attack of diarrhoea while on the tanker boom, but despite his discomfort, he elected to continue the mission. Having convinced John that he now felt much better, Buzz completed the air refuelling task and accelerated due south.

Since the French government had denied permission to over-fly, it was necessary to skirt the Iberian peninsula on the way into the Mediterranean. Carpenter and Murphy completed a second refuelling east of Gibraltar, before returning to high-Mach flight. After overflying the Suez Canal, they descended for their third tanker rendezvous over the Red Sea. However, the planned double-loop coverage of the collection area was interrupted by the ANS, which tried to initiate a preprogrammed turn prior to reaching the correct destination point (DP). Upon recognising the error, the crew flew the aircraft manually while trying to work out what had caused the 'glitch' in the autopilot's AutoNav function. As a result of this miscue, they overshot the turn point but completed the rest of the route and made their way back to the tankers for another Red Sea top-up. A fifth air refuelling was completed east of Gibraltar and one hour 30 minutes later they recovered '972 back in to Mildenhall after a 10-hour sortie.

The mission itself had generated considerable interest within the 9th SRW as well as at SAC Headquarters and in Washington. As a result, Buzz and John were greeted by a large number of colleagues as they stepped off the SR's boarding gantry (including Col Dave Young, the 9th SRW vice commander), who gave Buzz a brown SR-71 tie tack to commemorate the in-flight incident when, to misquote a well known phrase, 'the world fell out of Buzz's bottom'.

When the photo 'take' was processed at Mildenhall, it was of exceptional quality and the incident that had delayed the turn had yielded the most important information. That unexpected success made additional flights to the area unnecessary. Consequently, Rich Graham and Don Emmons returned '972 to Beale on 28 March.

A new detachment

To date, and with the exception of the Yemen sortie, these early Giant Reach missions were invariably used to gather Elint, as Photint opportunities were extremely limited due to the prevailing weather conditions in Northern Europe. To service the SR-71's requirements during these deployments, Headquarters SAC activated portions of the Mildenhall-based Mobile Processing Centre (MPC II), located in Hangar 538. These facilities enabled several of the SR-71's computer-driven subsystems to be programmed; the high-resolution radar data was also processed and a preliminary readout of the Elint collection was also conducted; a more

detailed Elint analysis was later carried out by the 9th RTS at Beale and the 544th Strategic Intelligence Wing at Offutt AFB, Nebraska. However, as the result of a conference convened at Headquarters SAC in mid-November 1978, Giant Reach missions from Mildenhall were about to receive a shot in the arm; the meeting (chaired by a representative from the DIA and including participants from SAC and USAF Headquarters, Headquarters USAF Europe (USAFE), and the Navy's Atlantic Command), unanimously agreed that the SR-71's high-resolution radar was the ideal sensor for monitoring Soviet subs. Consequently, included within the tasking order to monitor the 1979 spring troop rotation, was an additional requirement – that the SR-71 should also conduct Radint surveillance of the Soviet Navy's Northern Fleet. As a result of this additional tasking requirement, and after nearly two years of short TDY deployments, Detachment 4 (Det 4) of the 9th SRW was activated at RAF Mildenhall on 31 March, to support both Lockheed U-2R and SR-71 operations.

On 17 April, FERN 29 arrived at the newly created detachment, and over the next 15 days aircraft '979 completed the dual tasking requirements. The autumn troop rotation and sub surveillance was carried-out by '972, which arrived on 13 September as CUP 10. On 15 October it was positioned to RAF Lakenheath, while Mildenhall underwent essential runway maintenance. It continued its operational missions from this temporary home, eventually returning to Beale as ROOM 60, on 2 November, having remained in the UK for a record 50 days.

Poland

Throughout the summer of 1980 a series of strikes was organised by workers at the Lenin shipyard in Gdansk, Poland, in support of a dismissed colleague. At the end of August, an agreement was signed by Lech Walesa, the strike leader, and Mieczyslaw Jagielski, the deputy Prime Minister, providing independent unions with the right to strike, an easing of censorship and the release of political prisoners. A month later saw the creation of the 'Solidarity' union in communist Poland and in October the Polish Roman Catholic Church openly threw its support behind the union. However, hardliners within the Polish communist party accused Solidarity of abusing its new rights and the USSR, East Germany and Czechoslovakia called up military reservists. Fearing possible military intervention, US intelligence requested that the JCS direct an SR-71 to monitor the situation. As a result, '964 arrived at Mildenhall on 12 December and stayed for an unprecedented four months.

To further satisfy the Navy's requirement for Radint imagery of the Northern Fleet, SAC began a number of SR-71 Radint/Elint round-robin sorties from Beale to the Barents Sea (the first in 1979 and a further two in 1980). However, the ideal solution to these enhanced Giant Reach missions would be to permanently base two SR-71s at Mildenhall. Such a move would reduce mission response times and be much more cost effective, but further funding would be needed for new support facilities (a maintenance complex, two single-aircraft hangars, added fuel storage and an engine run-up 'hush house'). This it was estimated would cost about $14 million, which it was believed would be far too much for the necessary approval. Cost-cutting elements were therefore incorporated into the proposal, including recycled Beale hangars, a renovated Mobile Processing Centre (MPC) and 'civilian contract' maintenance. Such cost savings brought costs down to about $10 million. Missions were planned at a rate of ten per month – the actual requirement was greater, but this was suppressed from SAC HQ, which would then have insisted upon a three-aircraft complement,

which again would have escalated costs to a point that would have jeopardised the entire proposal. After some imaginative manoeuvring bordering on the inspirational, the SR-71 Program Element Manager (PEM) at the Pentagon finally managed to steer the Program Objective Memorandum (POM) through a political minefield where it leapt from 450th position in the order of priorities to 7th. Concurrences came in from all parties and Senior Crown had survived to fight another day in its new role from RAF Mildenhall.

Deployments to the Suffolk base continued throughout the 1980s, with the main 'collection areas' being the Barents and Baltic Seas, in support of US Navy intelligence requirements. The necessity to remain in international airspace at all times constrained the SR-71's flight profile when flying within the tight geographical confines of Northern Europe, which in turn required even higher levels of crew proficiency. For this reason newly qualified crews always flew their first operational missions in the Far East, with Det 1, at Kadena. In Europe, the aircraft's speed and bank angles were adjusted, often by a wide margin, in order to remain 'on the black-line'. For example, bank angles were generally flown at 35° (and restricted to a maximum of 45°), generating a turn radius of 70 nm (81 miles; 130 km) at Mach 3.2. Within Europe however, the aircraft's speed was often reduced to Mach 2.8, where a bank angle of 43° would reduce the turn radius to 40 nm (46 miles; 74 km). Outside air temperature also had an

With the offensive part of Operation El Dorado Canyon concluded, the first of Det 4's post-strike reconnaissance sorties became airborne even before the last of the F-111 bombers had landed back at Lakenheath. Conditions were not ideal for a Habu launch, but the primary aircraft suffered no problems and the air spare was not needed. (Paul F. Crickmore)

impact on the aircraft's performance; the temperature of the Arctic air mass at high altitude was often 10°C warmer than the norm (at -46.5°C, instead of -56.5°C), due to the shape and height of the troposphere; this could increase the compressor inlet temperature (CIT), by as much as 30°C, and with the CIT red-lined at 427°C, this was yet another factor that had to be monitored closely by the crew.

On 9 July 1983 British aviation enthusiasts 'manning' the many off-base vantage points at Mildenhall noted the arrival of aircraft '962, an aircraft that had 'pulled' TDY at the base on previous occasions. In fact the seven-hour operational flight from Beale to Mildenhall, via the Barents/Baltic areas had taken place in the Palmdale flight test aircraft '955. A false serial number had been applied to divert unwelcome attention away from a unique operational test deployment then underway. The detachable nose section of '955 was equipped with Loral's Advanced Synthetic Radar System (ASARS-1), a system that provided a quantum leap in radar resolution. With maritime data collected during

This OBC shot was taken by SR-71A '980 (TROMP 30), on 15 April 1986. It shows the damage inflicted on the Libyan air base at Benina by US Navy A-6 Intruders, and its resolution has been purposely degraded prior to release to the media to hide the system's true capability. (USAF)

Aircraft '964 leaves Mildenhall for the last time following the programme shutdown. Pilot Don Watkins and his RSO Bob Fowlkes brought the aircraft around for one last flypast over 'the Hall' for the assembled press and aircraft enthusiasts. (Paul F. Crickmore)

the inbound flight, another crew conducted a 2-hour 36-minute ASARS operational test sortie of land-based targets in East Germany nine days later. On 21 July a four-hour mission was chalked-up, with the final ASARS operational proving flight being conducted on 30 July, when '962 sic '955, completed a 7-hour 20-minute flight back to Beale, again via the Baltic and Barents Seas. The series of tests proved extremely successful and following further tests back at Palmdale, two production radar sets for the operational fleet were funded and deployed.

More Middle East missions

The early eighties brought with them a resurgence of Islamic fundamentalism, sparked off when Ayatollah Khomeini and his supporters declared Iran to be an Islamic Republic, a move that many western intelligence commentators agreed represented yet another potentially destabilising influence within the complex arena of Middle Eastern politics. During this period SR-71s from Mildenhall occasionally ventured into the eastern Mediterranean to monitor the movements of various contraband supplied by sympathetic states to Islamic Jihad warriors and key terrorist leaders as their small executive support aircraft slipped from one tiny desert airstrip to another.

One such SR-71 sortie took place on 27 July 1984, when, at 07:30, aircraft '979 departed Mildenhall bound for the Lebanon. Yet again, due to French 'politicking' with various Arab nations, overflight transit for access into the

Mediterranean was refused, necessitating entry via the Strait of Gibraltar. In addition, the flight was further complicated by inlet door and spike control problems, which meant that the pilot was forced to control the inlets and spikes manually. After two air refuellings and recycling all inlet switches, the 'glitch' still refused to clear; by this time the crew had already come so far that they reasoned they may as well press on. Flown in this configuration the aircraft's emergency operating procedures dictated that performance should be limited to Mach 3 and 70,000 ft (21336 m). The mission called for a single high-speed, high-altitude pass over the target area, which the crew completed. However, operating in the less fuel-efficient 'manual' inlet configuration, the run ended in a notably depleted fuel state. The RSO urgently contacted the tankers that were orbiting near the island of Crete and asked that they head east to meet the thirsty Habu. As BOYCE 64 descended, the pilot caught sight of the tankers 30,000 ft (9144 m) below and executed what he later described loosely as 'an extremely large variation of a barrel roll' and slid the SR in behind the tankers 'in no time flat'. It stayed on the boom some 12 to 15 minutes longer than normal in order to regain the preplanned fuel disconnect point. It then cleared the tanker, accelerated and cruise climbed back to Mildenhall. The flight (of nearly 7 hours duration), produced a 'take' of superb quality as the result of a cold front that covered the eastern Mediterranean, the very clear air delivering 'razor sharp' photographic imagery.

Following programme shutdown, Eric Schulzinger, with the help of friends in the 9th SRW, composed this memorable shot. Eleven SRs were collected together for the photograph, including 'the bastard' SR-71C which was placed in the background. (Lockheed Martin Skunk Works)

Lt Colonels Ed Yeilding and JT Vida established a coast-to-coast speed record of 1 hour 8 minutes on 6 March 1990 in SR-71A 64-17972. (USAF)

Det 4's commander, Col Jay Murphy, was especially proud of his crew's notable mission accomplishments, even though 'the book' dictated that words had to be spoken about flying a 'degraded' aircraft over a known Soviet SA-5 SAM site. However, like Jay, the National Photographic Interpretation Center (NPIC), back in Washington was also 'extremely pleased' with this 'most valuable take'.

Tension between the United States and much of the Arab world continued, and after a series of incidents, President Reagan's patience reached a violent end. On 15 April 1986 Operation Eldorado Canyon, a co-ordinated strike on targets in Libya by air elements of the US Navy and eighteen USAF F-111s from RAF Lakenheath, was mounted. SR-71 '980 (callsign TROMP 30) departed Mildenhall at 05:00 that same day, its mission to secure photographic imagery for post-strike bomb damage assessment. To achieve this it was necessary to overfly those targets hit earlier, but this time in broad daylight and with the sophisticated Libyan defence network on full alert. Such was the importance of the mission, that an air spare, in the form of aircraft '960 (TROMP 31), was launched at 06:15 in case the primary aircraft aborted with mechanical or sensor problems. In the event all aircraft systems, the two chine mounted Technical Objective Cameras (TEOCs) for spot coverage and the nose-mounted Optical Bar Cameras (OBC) for horizon-to-horizon coverage worked as advertised and '960 was not called upon to penetrate hostile airspace. Despite launches against '980, the SR-71 again proved that it could operate with impunity against SAM threats and at 09:35 TROMP 30 landed safely back at 'the Hall'. The mission's 'take' was processed in the MPC located within Hangar 538. It was then transported by a KC-135 (TROUT 99) to Andrews AFB, Maryland, where national-level officials were eagerly awaiting post-strike briefings.

Two further missions over Libya were conducted on 16 and 17 April, with minor route changes and different call signs being used. This intense period of reconnaissance activity scored many new 'firsts' for Det 4; the first occasion that both SRs were airborne simultaneously; the first time KC-10s had been used to refuel SR-71s in the European theatre; the first time that photos taken by the SR-71s were released to the press (although the source was never officially admitted and the image quality was purposely degraded to hide true capability). All in all, the missions were a great accomplishment by the Det's support personnel, under the command of ex-SR-71 RSO, Lt Col Barry MacKean.

Ironically, the Senior Crown programme was 'living on borrowed time' without an electro-optical backplate for the SR's camera system and a data-link system which would permit both camera and radar imagery to be down-linked in near real time. Eventually funds were appropriated for the development of Senior King, a secure data link via satellite, but its development would prove too late to save the SR-71 Blackbird.

Shutdown

By the late 1980s the list of those articulating an anti-SR-71 posture included a group of people as broad and varied as they were powerful. Dewain Andrews and Bob Fitch, serving on the Senate's House Permanent Select Committee on Intelligence (HPSCI), appeared to make the closure of the Senior Crown programme a personal crusade. Within the Air Force at that time detractors included Chief of Staff, General Larry Welch, Air Force Executive Officer General Dougan, CINCSAC General John Chain, Air Force Programme Requirements General Ron Fogleman, Chief of SAC Intelligence (SAC/IN) General Doyle, Col Tanner also (SAC/IN) and General Leo Smith of the Budget Review Board. As their assault got underway, the main thrust of their argument orientated itself around cost issues versus the 'marginal benefits' of operating the SR-71 over satellites; in addition, the

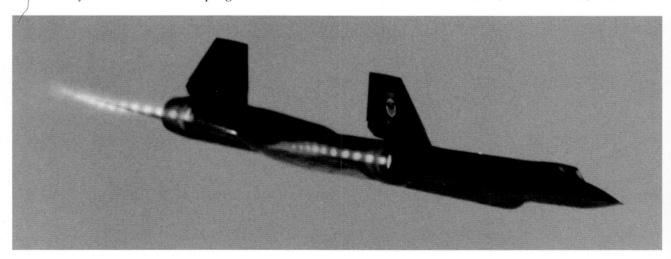

Following programme shutdown, aircraft '980 was positioned to Palmdale and given the NASA tail number 844. It went on to fly the Linear Aerospike SR-71 Experiment (LASRE) tests with a special pylon attached to its upper fuselage centreline and is now scheduled for display at NASA's Dryden Flight Research Center. (USAF)

Flying downwind with its undercarriage in transition for landing, aircraft '958 was photographed in the Beale circuit. The row of twelve hangars once provided homes for the operational Habus at Beale. (Lockheed Martin Skunk Works)

Pentagon contended that an air-breathing replacement was under development, and during a meeting on Capitol Hill, Welch testified (incorrectly) that the SR-71 had become vulnerable to SA-5 and SA-10 SAMs.

By 1988 it looked as though these combined efforts would be successful. But all was not quite lost: Admiral Lee Baggott, Commander in Chief, Atlantic (CINCLANT) still required SR-71 coverage of the Kola peninsula as there were no other systems available that were capable of meeting the Navy's requirements. He took the battle to retain the SR-71 in Europe right to the Joint Chiefs of Staff (JCS) and obtained funding for Det 4 for a further year. Meanwhile the SR-71 PEM and his action officer were able to secure a commitment from a staffer on the Senate Appropriations Committee for $46 million to keep both Kadena and Palmdale open for another year. Thereafter however, the antagonists got their way and what was to be the final flight of an SR-71 took place on 6 March 1990, when Ed Yeilding and JT Vida flew '972 on a west to east coast record-breaking flight of the United States, before landing at the Smithsonian National Aerospace Museum, Washington, DC,

where the aircraft was handed over for permanent display. With the SR-71 fleet retired from the inventory, three aircraft were placed in storage at Site 2, Palmdale; two A models and the sole surviving two-seater were loaned to NASA, while the remaining 13 aircraft (including the hybrid trainer designated SR-71C), were donated to various museums throughout the United States – despite more than forty members of Congress, together with many other well placed officials and senior officers voicing their concern over the decision.

During the course of the Gulf War, two requests were made to reactivate the Senior Crown programme, both however were turned down by the same Sec Def who had presided over the aircraft's shutdown a year earlier – Dick Cheney. That Desert Storm was an overwhelming success for coalition forces is beyond dispute; however there were lessons to be learned from the 41 day campaign, not least of which was the lack of timely reconnaissance material available to General Schwarzkopf's field commanders.

It was not until March/April 1994 that events in the international arena once more took a turn.

Relations between North Korea and the United States (at best always strained) reached a new low over the North's refusal to allow inspection of its nuclear facilities. At this point Senator Robert Byrd took centre stage; he, together with several members of the armed services and various members of Congress, contended that back in 1990 the Pentagon had consistently lied about the supposed readiness of a replacement for the SR-71. The motivation behind such comments did not appear to be the usual politicking, but one of genuine concern for the maintenance of a platform capable of survivable broad area synoptic coverage.

The campaigning and lobbying paid off as short-term provision was made for a modest, 'three plane SR-71 aircraft contingency reconnaissance capability', at a cost of $100 million, for fiscal year 1995 (FY95). Of the three SR-71As that were stored at Palmdale, only '967 was called to arms. The other A model to be re-commissioned was '971 which had been loaned to NASA, re-numbered 832 and regularly ground tested but never flown by its civilian caretakers. The pilot trainer SR-71B, together with the brand new flight simulator purchased just months before shut-down, would be shared by the Air Force and NASA, and in a further move to keep operating costs to a minimum the new detachment, designated Det 2, would, like the NASA operation, be based at Edwards AFB.

Aircraft reactivation began on 5 January 1995 with a fuel-leak evaluation of '967. Seven days later, at 11:26, NASA crew Steve Ishmael and Research Systems Operator Marta Bohn-Meyer got airborne from Edwards in '971 on a 26-minute ferry flight that terminated at Lockheed Martin's Skunk Works Plant 10 Building 602, Palmdale. Over the next three months ASARS, together with other sensors previously in storage at Luke AFB, Arizona, were installed. At 10:18 on 26 April, NASA crew Ed Schneider and Marta completed a 34-minute FCF in '971. A month later Ed, and Marta's husband, Bob Meyer, conducted '971's second and final FCF that lasted 2 hours 30 minutes. However, it took seven further check flights to wring out all the glitches in '967 the final one was successfully completed on 12 January 1996.

Three Air Force crews were selected to fly the aircraft, the plan being that two crews would always be 'Mission Ready' qualified and the third crew, 'Mission Capable'. While crew proficiency training got underway in the simulator and the 'B' model, Research and Development funds were used to develop and install the long overdue data link.

As the qualified USAF crews began to acquaint themselves with their aircraft, the on-going battle between the various factions supporting or against the resurrected programme came to a head. Exploiting a complex technical loop-hole in the legislation, antagonists asserted that it was technically illegal to operate the SR-71. Consequently, at 23:00 (Zulu) on 16 April 1996, a signal was despatched from the Pentagon, once again suspending all SR-71 ops with immediate effect. This was overturned when supporters serving on the Senate Appropriations Committee threatened to defeat the Intelligence Authorization Act for fiscal 1997. This would have halted all intelligence activities, not only

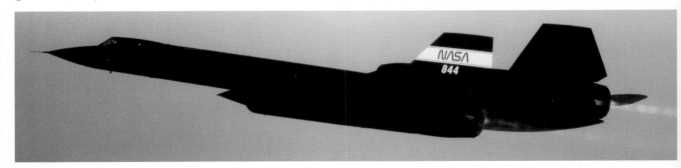

Aircraft '980 was flown for the first time by its new owner (NASA) on 24 September 1996. The pilot was Steve Ishmael and the RSO Marta Bohn-Meyer. NASA has used the SR-71 sparingly, but it has produced useful data during high-speed propulsion tests. (NASA)

LOCKHEED A-12, F-12 AND SR-71 BLACKBIRD

Following the limited USAF reactivation, NASA 832 reverted to its original Air Force serial number (64-17971) and undertook its first functional check flight on 26 June 1995. Similarly, '967 was reactivated and it is seen here refuelling from a KC-135T, callsign SLED 71. (Lt Col Blair Bozek)

within the USAF, but also the DIA, CIA, NSA, etc! Some $39 million was therefore allocated to the programme, $30 million for operations and maintenance and $9 million for procurement. Once again, expectations in Det 2 were running high as the next phase of sensor enhancement involving the development of an electro-optical backplate for the TEOCs got underway.

Unfortunately, the political prevarication and lobbying continued and on 10 October 1997, President Clinton line-item vetoed the Senior Crown programme – he simply crossed it off the budget – and everything drew to a halt. Routine maintenance work continued until 30 September 1999 (the end of the military fiscal year), after which the remaining monies ran out and Senior Crown finally succumbed. On 6 October 1999, Detachment 2 of the 9th Strategic Reconnaissance Wing was deactivated.

For 30 years the SR-71 had operated without being intercepted, over the most heavily fortified areas of the world. By 1981, over one thousand SA-2s had been launched against the aircraft; but due to its speed, altitude and sophisticated DEF systems, all missed.

The projection of military power, in the form of a carrier battle group, is a useful deterrent to potential conflict and underpins political rhetoric. Similarly, the SR-71's unique ability to overfly the capital of any potential enemy unmolested, gathering as it goes reconnaissance data, whilst laying down a triple sonic boom, reinforces military superiority and intent, in a manner that a state-run propaganda machine would find difficult to dismiss.

Today, the United States and the West are extremely reliant upon satellites for the collection of strategic reconnaissance data from otherwise 'denied' areas. The sickening events of 11 September 2001 vividly demonstrated the vulnerability of an open society to an attack, the like of which has not been witnessed since the Japanese Kamikaze attacks of World War II. It also demonstrated, in gut wrenching terms, what happens when intelligence agencies rely too heavily on a limited number of collection sources. Shortly after the attacks, various members of Congress wrote to SecDef Donald Rumsfeld, urging him to consider reactivating two SR-71As in a bid to bolster US reconnaissance-gathering capabilities. Alas, the only way of tracking well-trained terrorist cells is via an effective human intelligence (Humint), network. However, due to the various systems upgrades described earlier, the SR-71 is now in a unique position to make an unrivalled contribution to countering global terrorism, if President George W. Bush is serious about tackling states that arm, train, support or prepare for them weapons of mass destruction.

6. Design Accomplishments

The SR-71 was and remains a classic; students of this remarkable aircraft soon realise, when trying to describe its capabilities, that comparatives are rendered redundant. Invariably superlatives reign – it remains the fastest, highest-flying operational jet the world has ever seen. It operated, routinely, in the most challenging environment imaginable. In this particular context, the term 'challenging environment', has a number of different connotations. It was certainly a challenge for every member of its design team, no matter what their particular specialisation; Air Force crews and contractors that maintained this incredibly complex aircraft also echo those sentiments. Finally, SR-71 pilots and RSOs that participated in some of the most demanding and important strategic reconnaissance gathering missions of the Cold War will tell you that it was both challenging and supremely rewarding to have been associated with the programme.

General layout

The exterior of the SR-71 is characterised by an aft-body delta-wing with two large engine nacelles, each mounted at mid-semi span. Two all-moving vertical fins are located on top of each nacelle and canted inboard 15° from the vertical to reduce the aircraft's radar signature and to aid in controlling excess offset yaw-thrust during single-engine flight. A large, aft-moving inlet spike, or centre-body, protrudes forward from each engine nacelle, helping to regulate mass airflow to the two Pratt & Whitney J58 engines. Mission sensors were housed in a detachable nose section and in equipment bays located in the underside of the chine, which extended along both sides of the long fuselage fore-body. Wearing full pressure suits, the SR's crew of pilot and Reconnaissance Systems Officer (RSO) sit in tandem in separate cockpits in the forward fuselage.

Materials

In the near-vacuum conditions at 83,000 ft (25298 m), the ambient air pressure is about 0.4 psi (0.03 bar) and the temperature hovers around -55°C. However, cruising in afterburner at its design speed of Mach 3.2 – that is 1 mile (1.6 km) every 1.8 seconds and faster than a .30-calibre bullet, there remains enough air resistance to send airframe temperatures rocketing; on the skin around the cockpit areas these register 220°C – roughly equivalent to the hottest setting on a domestic cooker. The wing leading edges get hotter than a soldering iron and outside nacelle areas adjacent to the afterburner section reach a staggering 560°C. For this reason, thermodynamic factors influenced the design and construction of the SR-71 more than any other aircraft of the period. Only titanium and stainless steel could withstand operating in this 'thermal thicket', and as titanium weighs only half as much as the latter, 93 per cent of the SR-71's structural weight consisted of aged titanium B-120 VCA; the remaining 7 per cent – tail units and the triangular wedges that framed the outer edges of the aircraft – are of composite construction; made from a mixture of asbestos and epoxy, they provide the ability to withstand high-temperatures, while exhibiting radar-absorbent characteristics in order to reduce the aircraft's radar cross-section (RCS).

06932

U.S. AIR FORCE

Lockheed A-12

06936

FX-936

U.S. AIR FORCE

Lockheed YF-12A

06940

U.S. AIR FORCE

Lockheed M-21/D-21

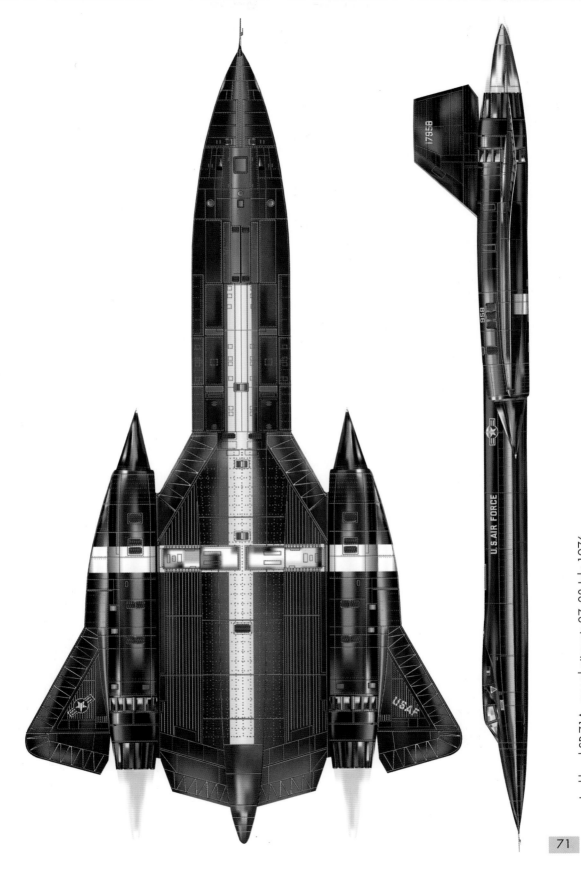

Lockheed SR-71A, record attempts 27–28 July 1976

The decision to use titanium represented a milestone in the continuing evolution of aviation materials and, by necessity, led to the invention and perfection of many new and different airframe assembly procedures. Initially, the titanium-aging process required 70 hours to achieve maximum strength, but careful processing techniques developed by the Skunk Works reduced this to 40 hours. Over-aging titanium results in brittleness and some early samples fell foul of this, shattering when dropped from desk height. Lockheed believed the problem to be hydrogen embrittlement produced during its heat treatment process; but despite the close co-operation of Lockheed's supplier, Titanium Metals Corporation, the case remained unproven and unresolved until Lockheed replaced its entire acid pickling (cleaning) facility with a unit identical to that used by TMC.

A rigorous quality control programme was introduced; for every batch of ten or more parts processed, three test samples were heat treated to the same level as those in the batch. One was then strength tested to destruction, another tested for

Each of the two main undercarriage struts has three wheels mounted on a hollow axle permitting any one wheel to be changed without removing the other two. The tyres are 32 ply, cost around $2,300 each, have a life averaging just 15 full-stop landings and are filled with nitrogen to a pressure of 415 psi (28.64 bar); their walls are impregnated with aluminium powder to help reflect airframe heat when retracted. (Paul F. Crickmore)

The Skunk Works' chief thermodynamicist on the SR-71, Ben Rich, once said that wherever possible he used the KISS formula – Keep It Simple, Stupid. Here a stand-off clip was used to provide a heat shield between the outer skin and heavier sub-structure, but maintained structural integrity. (Lockheed Martin Skunk Works)

formability and the third held in reserve in case reprocessing should be required. With more than 13 million titanium parts manufactured, data was stored on all but a few early samples.

Titanium is a metal with several idiosyncrasies and it was not long before Lockheed became well acquainted with them; for example, it is not compatible with chlorine, fluorine or cadmium. So a line drawn on a sheet of titanium with a Pentel pen will eat a hole through it in about 12 hours; perhaps not surprisingly, all Pentel pens were called in off the shop floor. Early spot-welded panels produced during the summer had a habit of failing, while those put together in the winter lasted indefinitely. Through diligent detective work, it was discovered that to prevent the formation of algae in summer, the Burbank water supply is heavily chlorinated. Thereafter, all titanium parts were washed in distilled water. During prolonged heat soak tests, bolt heads began dropping off various installations; this it was discovered, was caused by tiny cadmium deposits left after cadmium-plated spanners had been used to apply torque. All cadmium-plated spanners were then removed from tool boxes.

Lockheed awarded the Wyman Gordon Company a $1 million contract to fund a research programme into methods of forming complex structural pieces from titanium, such as the gear legs and engine nacelle rings. The result was a unique hot forging process that utilised a

50,000-ton press to force the metal to the desired shape. Lockheed designed high-speed cutting tools that were then used to machine such items. Initially, a drill bit could cut just 17 holes in the hard metal before it was ruined; however, by the end of the programme Lockheed ADP had developed bits that could bore 100 holes and then be successfully resharpened. The Skunk Works even developed a cutting fluid which, as well as eliminating the corrosive effects of many similar fluids, permitted metal removal at double the normal rates. The parts were then pickled – to prevent them from going under-gauge while in the acid baths, metal measuring gauges 0.002 in (0.051 mm) thicker were used. After cleaning, a pre-assembly inspection was carried out and the relevant segments assembled on spot-welding

machines. To prevent oxidisation, welding was conducted with the parts placed in specially constructed chambers enclosing a neutral, nitrogen gas environment.

During a test undertaken to study thermal effects on large titanium wing panels, a sample 4 ft x 6 ft (1.22 m x 1.83 m) was heated to the computed heat flux expected during flight; it resulted in the specimen warping into a totally unacceptable shape. Kelly Johnson overcame the problem by pressing chord-wise corrugations into the outer skins. Upon reaching the designed heat rate, the corrugations merely deepened a few thousandths of an inch and on cooling, returned to their original shape. Kelly commented at the time that some accused him of 'trying to make a 1932 Ford Trimotor go Mach 3', but the concept worked well. Another thermodynamic challenge to overcome was the problem caused by differential heating received by various parts of interconnecting structure. For example, from a uniform start temperature of 27°C, 8 minutes after acceleration a wing spar cap would reach 77°C, the spar web 102°C and the wing skin 177°C; it took another 16 minutes before all three components were within 8°C of one another. The problem therefore was how to attach a thin sheet of titanium to a much bulkier sub-structure, without the former buckling and tearing. As ever, the Skunk Works developed an innovative solution; a stand-off clip provided the anchor mechanism to the sub-structure, while also creating a heat shield between the skin and adjacent components.

The SR-71 was painted black, not to make it look sinister or menacing, but in an attempt to further reduce airframe temperatures. As stated in Kirchoff's law of radiation, a good absorber is a good emitter, and a good absorber is a black body. Since convective heating decreases with increasing altitude, and radiation is independent of height, it was useful to harness this radiation component in order to cool the airframe when cruising above 70,000 ft (21336 m). Experiments demonstrated that black paint provided an emissivity value of 0.92 compared to 0.38 for bare titanium; in addition, it was estimated that a black 'overcoat'

While 'hooked-up' to the refuelling boom, in addition to the transfer of the much-needed fuel, a secure intercom link is established between the SR and tanker. (Paul F. Crickmore)

Lockheed SR-71A, RAF Mildenhall 24 October–16 November 1977

Lockheed SR-71A Speed Record, 6 March 1990

Lockheed SR-71A, Beale AFB 1990

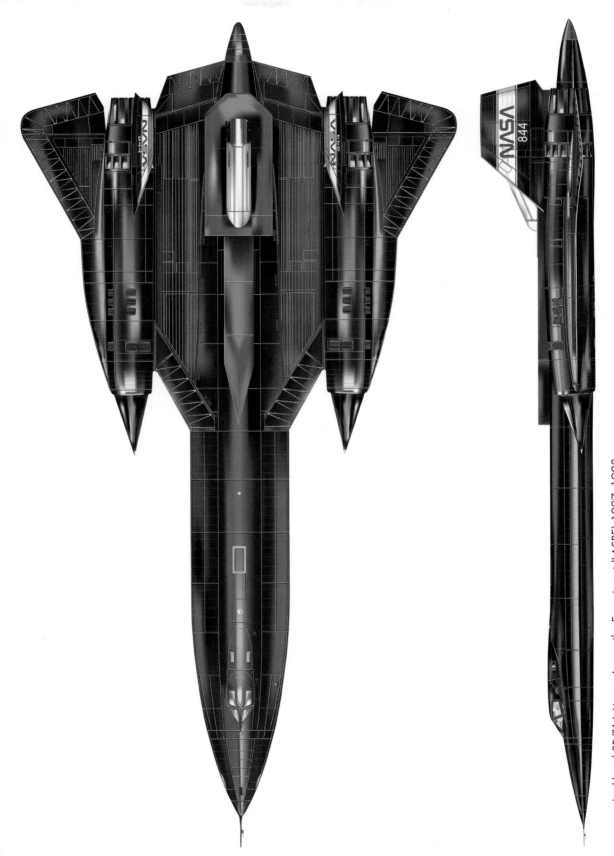

Lockheed SR-71A Linear Aerospike Experiment (LASRE) 1997–1998

When tanking from a KC-135 in warmer climes, it was often necessary for the SR-71 pilot to engage 'min burner' on one engine while on the boom, in order to take onboard the last 10,000 lb (4536 kg) of fuel. This additional thrust was needed to compensate for the added aerodynamic drag generated by the Habu as it approached maximum weight. (Paul F. Crickmore)

would actually reduce temperatures by between 15 and 30°C and this, it was felt, was well worth the 60-lb (27-kg) weight penalty incurred. Finally, when cruising at the inky-black altitudes of near space, black also helped to reduce the aircraft's visual signature when operating over 'denied airspace', while some sources also suggest that the paint may have had anti-radar qualities.

Powerplant

The Pratt & Whitney JT11D-20 (US military designation J58) powers the SR-71. Its stretched design criteria, particularly the requirement to operate at high Mach numbers and their associated large air-flow turn-down ratio, led to the development of a unique variable-cycle engine, later known as a bleed bypass engine – a concept conceived by Pratt & Whitney's Robert Abernathy. To solve the problems associated with the high compressor inlet temperatures encountered during high-Mach cruising speeds, the J58's bleed-bypass system diverts some air from the fourth stage of the nine-stage single spool axial-flow compressor, and passes it through six low-compression ratio bypass ducts. This process sharply reduces airflow pressures across the rear stages of the compressor assembly, preventing them from choking with high-velocity airflow; it also prevents the front stages from stalling, due to low-mass airflow. The ducted air is then

introduced to the turbine exhaust, near the front of the afterburner, at the same static pressure as the main flow, thereby reducing exhaust gas temperature and producing almost as much thrust per pound of air as the main flow which has passed through the rear compressor, the burner section and the turbine. To further minimise the risk of stalling the front stages of the fan blades at low engine speeds, the engine incorporates movable inlet guide vanes (IGVs) to help guide airflow to the compressor. During take-off and acceleration to intermediate supersonic speeds, these remain in the 'axial' position in order to optimise available thrust. A change to the 'cambered' position occurs at compressor inlet temperatures (CITs) of between 85 and 115°C, to ensure that the CIT remains within limits – the compressor temperature has a maximum limitation of 427°C. If the IGVs fail to transition to the 'cambered' position, then the flight must be aborted.

When operating at cruising speeds, the turbine inlet temperature rises to 1,100°C. This presented Pratt & Whitney with one of its greatest challenges, and one that was eventually overcome by Joseph Moore, a materials engineer at the Florida Research and Development Center, who perfected a special high-temperature alloy for use in both the first and second stage of the J58's turbine, known as 'Astralloy'.

The main and reduction gearboxes are mounted beneath the diffuser section of each engine and are mechanically linked to the engine's compressor section. The main gearbox is connected to an external drive-shaft for starting the engine; while the reduction gearbox provides mechanical power to the airframe-mounted Accessory Drive System (ADS), which includes a constant-speed drive, linked to a 60-kVA electrical generator, two hydraulic pumps and a fuel circulating pump.

Fuel system

The extremely high airframe temperatures encountered by the SR-71 during high-Mach cruise completely ruled out the use of standard JP-4 as its fuel source, as it had to be carried in 'wet' tanks integral to the wing structure and therefore subject to massive heating. Instead, a bespoke fuel was designed specifically for the SR-71 and known as JP-7. It was developed by Pratt & Whitney, in partnership with Ashland, Shell and Monsanto and remained stable despite the high-temperature environment. It is used first as a hydraulic fluid to activate the main and afterburner fuel nozzles before being injected into the fuel burners at over 350°C and 130 psi (8.97 bar). Such high fuel burn temperatures presented the design team with yet another problem; standard electrical plugs were incapable of igniting the fuel. This was overcome by developing a unique chemical ignition system (CIS), involving the chemical tri-ethyl borane (TEB). Extremely flash sensitive when oxidised, the TEB is carried in a small tank onboard the aircraft and used to start or re-start the engines and afterburners on the ground or in the air. To ensure that the system remains inert when not in operation, gaseous nitrogen is used to pressurise the TEB tank and power the piston that injects it into the burner cans during the ignition process, regardless of engine operating conditions. As fuel is burnt, gaseous nitrogen is also used to pressurise the fuel tanks to prevent them from being crushed as the aircraft descends to lower levels to either air-refuel or land. For this purpose, liquid nitrogen is carried aloft in two 398-US gal (105-litre) dewars that are located either side of the front nose gear, in the wheel well. Each time the SR-71 air-refuels, the nitrogen gas in the fuel cells is vented overboard; range is therefore governed by the number of times the aircraft can be refuelled before the liquid nitrogen supply becomes depleted.

Development of a durable fuel tank sealant was an on-going problem; as the aircraft cruises at high Mach, it expands 3 in (7.62 cm) in length due to thermodynamic heating. Upon descending to air-refuel, the airframe cools, a process that is considerably speeded up as fuel at -50°C is pumped into the jet's tanks from either a KC-135 Stratotanker or KC-10 Extender tanker at 5,000 lb (2268 kg) per minute. This cycle of events was

Pratt & Whitney's aero engine designers were well equipped for the daunting task of developing an engine capable of coping with the vast range of ambient air temperatures, pressures and volumes demanded by the A-12 – the result was a classic, the J58. (Lockheed Martin Skunk Works)

Lockheed SR-71A, NASA.

Lockheed SR-71A with 'Dolby Noise Reduction' logo on tail.

Lockheed SR-71A. Among the last to be retired.

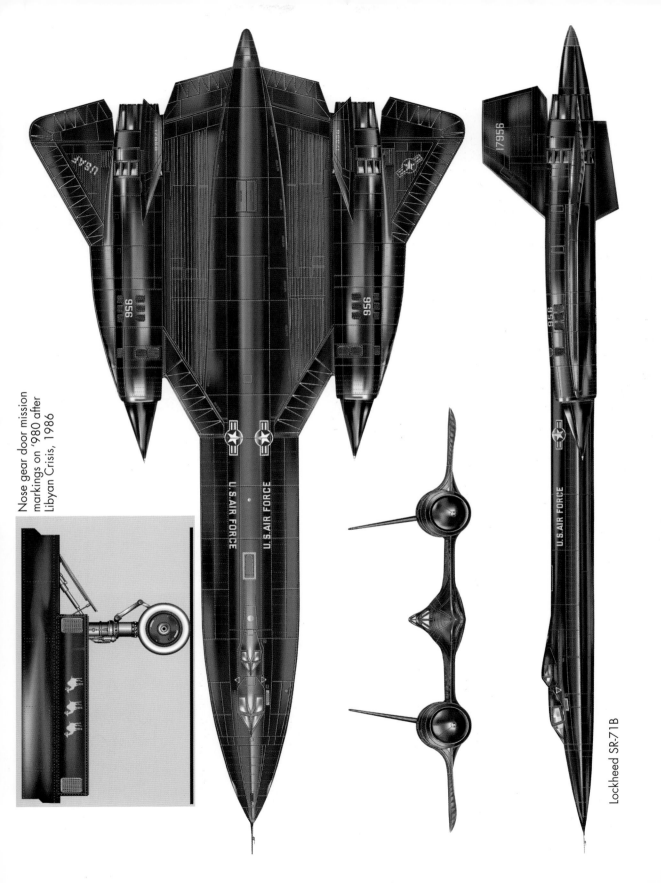

Nose gear door mission markings on '980 after Libyan Crisis, 1986

Lockheed SR-71B

The so-called 'Big Tail' conversion on '959 first flew on 11 December 1975, the objective being to increase sensor capacity/capability. Note the window behind which an OBC unit could be carried. The modification was not used operationally. (Lockheed Martin Skunk Works)

repeated five or six times during an extended US Air Force mission and many more times during the period between major maintenance overhauls. The pounding taken by the silicon-based sealant invariably led to it cracking, causing fuel to leak from numerous gaps.

Air Inlet Control System (AICS)

The SR-71 also boasts a unique, highly efficient air inlet system that supplements thrust via three components: an asymmetric, mixed-compression, variable-geometry inlet; the J58 engine; and a convergent/divergent, blow-in-door ejector nozzle. The AICS regulates the massively varying internal airflow throughout the aircraft's entire flight envelope, ensuring that the engines receive air at both the correct velocity and pressure.

To satisfy the J58's voluminous appetite for air during operations at ground idle, taxiing and take-off, the centrebody spikes are positioned fully forward, allowing an uninterrupted flow to the engine compressor. Supplementary flow is also provided through six forward bypass doors, plus a reverse flow is set-up through exit louvres on the spikes' centrebody and a set of variable-area 'inlet-ports' that are regulated by an external slotted band, which draws air in from two sets of doors. The task of operating these doors was initially manually controlled by the pilot, but was later accomplished automatically by a Digital Automatic Flight Inlet Control System (DAFICS)

Bob Gilliland was Lockheed's chief test pilot on the SR-71 programme. His personal callsign was DUTCH 51. (Lockheed Martin Skunk Works)

computer. Positioning of the electrically operated, hydraulically actuated spike is also controlled by the DAFICS. Operating together, the forward bypass doors and the centrebody spike are used to control the position – just aft of the inlet throat – of the normal shockwave created in flight. To optimise inlet efficiencies, the shock wave is captured and held inside the converging/diverging nozzle, just behind the narrowest part of the throat, thereby achieving the maximum possible pressure rise across the normal shock.

Once airborne, the forward bypass doors close automatically as the undercarriage is retracted. At Mach 1.4 the doors begin to modulate, again automatically, to obtain a pre-programmed ratio between 'dynamic' pressure at the inlet cowl on one side of the throat and 'static' duct pressure on the other side. Upon reaching 30,000 ft (9144 m),

SR-71B '956 was photographed flying with NASA number 831. Note the vortices streaming off the wing leading edges, as well as the still-wet staining behind the open inflight-refuelling receptacle. (NASA)

the inlet spike unlocks, and at Mach 1.6 begins a rearward translation, achieving its fully aft position of 26 in (66 cm) at Mach 3.2 – the inlets' most efficient speed. As the spike moves aft, the 'capture-air-stream-tube-area' increases by 112 per cent, while the throat restriction decreased by 46 per cent of its former size.

A peripheral 'shock trap' bleed slot (positioned around the outer circumference of the duct, just forward of the throat and set at two boundary layer displacement thicknesses), 'shaves off' 7 per cent of the stagnant inlet airflow and stabilises the terminal (normal) shock. It is then rammed across the engine's bypass plenum through 32 shock trap tubes spaced at regular intervals around the circumference of the shock trap. As this compressed, tertiary air travels down the secondary bypass passage, it firmly closes the suck-in doors and cools the exterior of the engine casing before being exhausted through the ejector nozzle. Potentially turbulent boundary layer air is removed from the surface of the centrebody spike at the point of its maximum diameter and then ducted, through the spike's hollow support struts, before being dumped overboard, through nacelle exit louvres. The aft bypass doors are opened at mid-Mach to minimise the aerodynamic drag that results from dumping air overboard through the forward bypass doors.

Unstarts

By carefully dove tailing all the above parameters, the inlet is able to generate internal duct pressures of 18 psi (1.24 bar); when this is considered against the ambient air pressure at 82,000 ft (24994 m) of just 0.4 psi (0.03 bar), it is immediately apparent that this extremely large pressure gradient is capable of producing a similarly large forward thrust vector. In fact, at Mach cruise, this accounts for no less than 54 per cent of the total thrust being produced; a further 29 per cent is produced by the ejector, while the remaining 17 per cent is generated by the J58 engine. If however, airflow disturbances disrupt this delicate pressure-balancing trick, it is equally easy to appreciate the effects that such excursions would have upon the

aircraft. This brings us to yet another of the SR-71's unique idiosyncrasies, the 'unstart'. These aerodynamic disruptions occurred when the normal shock wave was 'belched' forward from the inlet throat, causing an instant drop in the inlet pressure and thrust. With each engine positioned at mid-semi span, the shock wave departure manifested itself in a vicious yaw in the direction of the 'unstarted' engine; sometimes these were so strong that crewmembers would have their helmets knocked against the cockpit canopy framing. Recovery for such an incident involved an automatic, computer-sequenced, inlet restart. This involved the spike being driven forwards and the forward bypass doors opening to recapture and reposition the shock wave. The spike then returned to its correct position, followed by the bypass doors, which reconfigured the inlet to its optimum performance. Unstarts were a regular feature of early SR-71 flights, but as computer software improved, the DAFICS was able to achieve near-perfect inlet airflow control which practically rid the jet of its unstart problems.

Stability Augmentation System

The SR-71's centre of gravity (cg) is automatically moved aft during acceleration to high-Mach flight, to reduce trim drag and improve elevon authority in both the pitch and roll axes. The fuselage chine produces lift forward of the cg, which has the effect of destabilising the aircraft in the pitch axis and reduces aft cg travel, resulting in low static margins of stability and safety. In short, this means that the aircraft operated on the edge of controllability. Additionally, the chine has an adverse aerodynamic effect on the aircraft when performing sideslip manoeuvres at cruise angles of attack (AoA, or 'alpha') (approximately 6° of positive alpha, i.e. the aircraft tends to adopt a slightly nose-up attitude). This, coupled with low aerodynamic damping – inherent with flight at high altitudes – conspires to cause the SR-71 to be only marginally stable in both pitch and yaw at high Mach.

Control in this delicate, but critical, corner of the flight envelope is achieved by the aircraft's elevons and rudders. These are worked through an automatic flight control system (AFCS), which in turn is controlled via the DAFICS computers. The AFCS consists of three subsystems; a stability augmentation system (SAS); an autopilot; and a Mach trim system. As the co-ordinating system, the AFCS provides pitch, roll and yaw stabilisation via the flight control surfaces. Eight rate-sensing gyros detect divergence from stable flight and together with three lateral accelerometers, also provide motion-sensing signals that are applied to the multi-redundant SAS circuits in the DAFICS. Control over the AFCS is provided to the pilot via 'Pitch SAS', 'Roll SAS' and 'Yaw SAS' switches, located on the right-console panel. In addition to responding to the signals from DAFICS, the servos can also be activated by direct stick and rudder pedal inputs.

The autopilot features two separate 'hold functions': pitch and roll. Pitch control is achieved via the basic 'Attitude Hold', 'Knots Equivalent Airspeed (KEAS) Hold', or 'Mach Hold' modes. In roll, control is exercised via the basic 'Roll Attitude Hold', 'Heading Hold', or auto-steering 'AutoNav' modes; this latter mode is programmed to obey heading commands from the astro-inertial navigation system (ANS). When the autopilot is engaged, the aircraft is held in the roll attitude established at the time of engagement. With AutoNav selected, the autopilot controls roll to ensure that the aircraft adheres to the predetermined navigation track that the ANS accurately maintains. During operational sorties the aircraft was invariably flown in this mode to ensure that it remained stable and on an accurate track while the onboard sensors were activated.

The Mach trim system provides speed stability up to Mach 1.5, while the aircraft is either accelerating or decelerating – a period during

Following a limited reactivation, NASA 832 reverted to its original Air Force serial number ('971) and undertook its first functional check flight on 26 June 1995. It is shown here on a 2-mile, ILS final approach for landing on Runway 25 at Air Force Plant 42, Palmdale. (Jim Ross/NASA)

During a project codenamed Tagboard, two A-12s were modified to carry a D-21 remotely piloted drone and were re-designated M-21 (M standing for mother and D for daughter, thereby making a so-called Mother/Daughter combination). The 11,000-lb (4989-kg) D-21 was powered by a Marquardt RJ-43-MA-11 ramjet that developed 34,000 lb st (151.20 kN). (Lockheed Martin)

which the autopilot cannot be engaged. It compensates via the pitch trim actuator, for the aircraft's propensity to 'tuck' nose-down while accelerating through the Mach and rise, nose-up, while decelerating.

Astro Inertial Navigation System

Reconnaissance-gathering missions conducted by the SR-71 took it to some of the most politically sensitive areas of the world. It was therefore essential that it should be equipped with the most accurate navigation system available – particularly bearing in mind that it would be flying at a velocity of 3,000 ft (914 m) per second! The Nortronics Division Astro Inertial Navigation System, used in the Skybolt air-to-surface missile, was modified for use in the SR-71 as the NAS-14V2. Producing a terminal error accuracy of less than 0.5 miles (0.8 km) after covering distances the equivalent of more than half-way around the world, it was considered by some to be the most outstanding piece of equipment to come out of the entire Senior Crown programme. The ANS combined data from an inertial platform with a time datum supplied from a chronometer that was accurate to within 5 milliseconds. Position 'updating' was achieved automatically by astro-tracking, at any one time, six of the 52 most prominently visible stars, for navigation purposes, by day or night. The stars were computer-catalogued in an ephemeris memory that could be used for continuous cross-checking for track position referencing. Scanning the celestial bodies sequentially, through a pre-programmed tracker

mechanism mounted on a gimballed platform on top of the nav unit, it provided passive, refined location information.

When the autopilot was coupled to the ANS through the AutoNav function switch, the aircraft could be flown automatically and precisely on a predetermined flight path. The pre-planned route (worked out by highly experienced navigators) was electronically loaded via a Milar tape into the ANS's computer memory, a few hours prior to take-off. Inflight modifications could be made by the RSO using his Control and Display panel. During flight, the computer-sequenced plan directed the aircraft from one destination point (DP) to the next. Two further features of the ANS included ground reference position updating through the forward-looking view sight and sensor monitoring by reference to control point (CP) actions; CPs were predetermined track points programmed into the ANS that would activate or deactivate reconnaissance sensors; they served to alert the RSO that the system was about to turn on, that the system had functioned correctly, and that programmed activities were being automatically carried out. The ANS was backed up by a Singer-Kearfott (SKN2417) INS.

Velocity/Height System

The Velocity/Height (V/H) System produced information scaled electrically to represent the angular rate of motion between the aircraft and the terrain below. Signal sources for the system were the ANS and the V/H indicator in the RSO's cockpit. These signals were scaled at 0.2 volts (DC)

Standard operating procedure called for the SR-71 to launch on a light fuel load. This ensured that the aircraft was more manageable in the circuit should a malfunction require an abort and return to base. It also meant that the first order of business after take-off was usually to RV with a tanker. With JP-7 fuel oozing from numerous cracks in its fuel tank sealant, this freshly topped-up aircraft breaks boom-contact and eases further aft of the tanker. With both 'burners on, the aircraft then climbs to 33,000 ft (10058 m) before performing a 'dipsy doodle' manoeuvre where it descends at 2,500 ft (762 m) per minute and 'punches' through the sound barrier. A 450-kt (518-mph; 834-km/h) climb is then established and maintained up to Mach 2.6; thereafter a bleed schedule is followed, where 10 kt (11.5 mph; 7 km/h) is traded for an increase of 0.1 Mach. This ends with the aircraft arriving at 390 kt (449 mph; 723 km/h) and Mach 3.2 at about 78,000 ft (23774 m). (Paul F. Crickmore)

'targets of interest'. A manual exposure control panel also enabled the RSO to remotely control camera exposure settings in order to take account of various lighting conditions (brightness and reflectivity). This was graduated in degrees of sun angle with reference indices for low, normal, high and very high terrain reflectivity. Such changes were made by regulating DC voltage between 10 and 38 volts for sun angle settings between 5 and 90°, producing a kind of 'electronic aperture'.

Crew survival systems

Air Force regulation 60-16 requires pressure suits to be worn when flying above 50,000 ft (15240 m). The reason for this is that entry into this abnormal environment can cause many physiological problems that, if left unchecked, would kill the crew in minutes. During ascent, for example, a reduction in the partial pressure of oxygen will cause hypoxia, in an unprotected subject, above 25,000 ft (7620 m). Progressive cardiorespiratory and neurological effects trigger such symptoms as euphoria, loss of judgement and impaired memory. If unchecked, semiconsciousness and unconsciousness follow, with death resulting 4 or 5 minutes later. Also above 25,000 ft, decompression sickness (DCS) develops, due to the reduction of ambient air pressure. It is acquired with increasing rapidity and severity the higher the altitude. The condition results from the evolution of nitrogen gas bubbles from body fluids as the pressure falls, (much like the bubbles

per milliradian per second and produced reference information for the various reconnaissance sensors on the aircraft. Another device aiding surveillance interpretation was the sensor event/frame-count system. This correlated time, position, altitude and heading when the 'close look' cameras or Technical Objective Cameras (TEOCs) were in operation. The system used the ANS Mission Recorder System and a signal sensor processor to convert event input signals into 6 millisecond-wide event-marker-pulses, that were monitored by the ANS. On receiving an event-marker-pulse, the ANS activated a frame-count register associated with a particular sensor. This data (with precise location information), was recorded by the Mission Recorder System.

The RSO had the ability to manually operate and control all reconnaissance system sensors, despite the fact that these were normally fully pre-programmed for automatic turn on/turn off, and for changing 'look angles' to many different points, in order to frame hundreds of separate

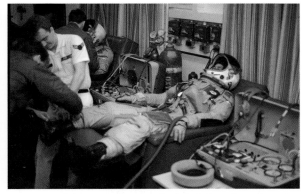

generated in a carbonated drink bottle when its top is removed). Joint pain (the 'bends'), chest pain, skin itching and neurological manifestations may develop alone or together, the last being more serious and potentially fatal.

Gas-containing body cavities – the lungs, gut, sinuses, etc, will increase in volume on ascent and contract on descent. Most of these problems are self-righting via the body's orifices; however, gas within the small gut is not free to escape and expansion can cause abdominal pain. To help reduce such symptoms operational crews ate high-protein meals prior to flight. During descent, considerable pain can arise if pressure in the middle ear cavities and sinuses cannot be equalised; for this reason crews undergo routine medicals prior to flight, and should a slight cold or throat infection be detected they are grounded until the condition has cleared.

Were the crew to be subjected to the outside air temperature prevailing at 80,000 ft (24384 m), they would undoubtedly risk local or general cold injury (frostbite and hypothermia respectively). To protect the crew from these effects, the cockpit is pressurised and pressure suits are worn. Within the cockpit, pressurisation is allowed to fall during ascent from sea level to 8,000 ft (2438 m); it then remains constant to 25,000 ft (7620 m). At these altitudes the ambient air pressure falls from 10.9 psi (0.75 bar) to 5.9 psi (0.41 bar) respectively, giving rise to a pressure differential of 5 psi (0.34 bar). This maximum figure is maintained by the aircraft's pressurisation system throughout the flight profile, which ensures that the fuselage is

The S901 silver pressure suit (left), was replaced by a white variant in the early seventies. (Paul F. Crickmore Collection)

not subjected to unduly high pressure gradients, which in turn means that construction weight can be reduced. However, in the event of rapid decompression or ejection, it means that the crew must wear full pressure suits to survive.

Like most other systems in the SR-71, these too evolved during the life of the programme; initially the David Clark S901J suit was issued to SR-71 crewmembers however this was replaced in 1974 by the S1030 suit. Manufactured by the same company, it incorporated state of the art textiles and was both more durable and comfortable. Its four layers consist of an outer coverall of Dacron which is durable, tear and fire resistant and coloured 'Old Gold'. A restraint/joint layer holds the suit together through restraint lines and acts as

The layout and instrumentation of an SR-71 front cockpit betrays its early-1960s design vintage. Rumours of the existence of a new-generation hypersonic reconnaissance platform abound, but the flaws in US intelligence exposed during Operation Enduring Freedom suggest that such an aircraft either does not exist, does not work, or is not yet ready for service. It is interesting to consider what might have been, if the SR-71 had been through the kind of avionics and sensor upgrade programmes that other USAF aircraft have enjoyed. (Paul F. Crickmore)

a pressure boundary; a third 'bladder' layer performs rather like a tyre inner tube and is made of polyurethane; finally, an inner scuff layer protects the all important bladder layer from scuffing against other clothing and the urine collection device (UCD). An optional thermal layer can be worn inside the suit, but this is usually discarded in favour of more comfortable long cotton underwear that is worn inside out, to prevent its seams from pressing into the skin.

The suit was built in 12 sizes and assumed the seated position when pressurised in order to aid cockpit mobility. Gloves completed the pressure seal and were attached via wrist hinges. The boots featured heel retraction strips that were connected by cable to the ejection seat on entry to the cockpit.

The complete pressure suit system cost about $30,000 a copy and lasted 10–12 years, undergoing a complete strip-down overhaul every five years and a thorough inspection every 90 days or 150 hours.

A modified Lockheed C-2 ejection seat, originally designed for the F-104, is fitted in the SR-71 and is designated as the Lockheed ADP SR-1 or F-1 stabilised ejection seat. It has zero speed/zero altitude capability and retains the crewmember in the seat if above 15,000 ft (4572 m) and inflates the pressure suit to protect the individual against the pressure differential. On reaching 15,000 ft, an aneroid barometer unblocks, causing seat separation and usual parachute deployment sequencing to continue.

Appendix 1. NASA Operations

In 1967 a deal was struck between NASA and the USAF, whereby the former was given access to early A-12 wind tunnel data in exchange for providing a small team of highly skilled engineers to work on the SR-71 flight test programme. Under the leadership of Gene Matranga, the team, from the NASA Flight Research Center (FRC) at Ames, was engaged on various stability and control aspects of the SR-71 at Edwards. This work helped speed the SR-71 into the inventory and led to the

establishment of a close working relationship between the Air Force and NASA.

The Office of Advanced Research Technology viewed the A-12/F-12 programme as a superb technical achievement, offering a potentially rich source of flight data applicable to future commercial supersonic transports (SSTs). With funds left over from the X-15 and cancelled XB-70 programmes, NASA signed a memorandum of understanding with the Air Force on 5 June 1969,

NASA utilised two YF-12s as illustrated, and an SR-71A (referred to as a YF-12C, for political reasons), for various high-altitude, high-Mach experiments. The early test team is pictured, from left to right, Ray Young, Fitz Fulton, Don Mallick and Vic Horton. (NASA)

The flight crew chosen to operate the NASA SR-71s in the 1990s were, from top to bottom, Rogers Smith, Ed Schneider, Bob Meyer and his wife, Marta Bohn-Meyer. (NASA)

which permitted it access to the two remaining YF-12s then in storage. It was agreed that NASA would pay for all operational expenses and Aerospace Defense Command (ADC) would supply maintenance and logistic support after both aircraft were fully instrumented. Phase One of the programme got underway when, on 11 December 1969, the first YF-12 to fly in three years climbed away from Edwards. This first phase was controlled by the Air Force, and consisted of developing procedures establishing limitations for command and control, and for working out possible bomber penetration tactics against an interceptor with the YF-12's capabilities. It was terminated on 24 June 1971, during the closing stages of the 63rd flight of 60-6936, which had been used throughout the tests by the Air Force. Lt Col Jack Layton and systems operator, Maj. Bill Curtis were approaching the traffic pattern before recovery back at Edwards when a fire broke out as a result of a fuel line fatigue fracture. The flames quickly enveloped the entire aircraft and while on base leg, both crewmembers safely ejected; '936 crashed into the middle of the dry lake bed and was totally destroyed.

While the YF-12s were being readied for flight, Donald L. Mallick and Fitzhugh L. Fulton Jr, the two NASA pilots who were to fly most of Phase

Two of the programme, were checked out in the Air Force SR-71B. Later, Victor Horton and Ray Young, the two NASA back-seaters, were checked out by Lt Col Bill Campbell in a YF-12 and the civilian programme began. Utilisation of the high-speed platform proved high, since NASA engineers at Langley were interested in aerodynamic experiments and testing advanced structures. The Lewis Research Establishment wanted to study propulsion, while Ames concentrated on inlet aerodynamics and the correlation of wind tunnel and flight-test data. In addition the aircraft was used to support various specialised experimentation packages. Taken together it was hoped that problems 'worked around' during the early test programme could be designed out of any future commercial SST venture, thereby avoiding expensive mistakes.

After the 22nd flight of '935 on 16 June 1970, the aircraft was grounded for nine months for instrumentation changes. Following a Functional Check Flight (FCF) on 22 March 1971, four flights were flown without the folding ventral fin, to assess directional stability up to Mach 2.8.

NASA needed more aircraft, therefore on 16 July 1971, the Air Force supplied an SR-71A (Article 2002, serial 64-17951). Throughout its life, this aircraft had been involved in the contractor flight test programme, but due to sensitivities, the Air Force stipulated that it should only be used for propulsion testing; in addition, it was given a new serial number (60-6937) and was referred to throughout the NASA test programme as a YF-12C; its first flight under new ownership occurred on 24 May 1972.

During various studies, it was discovered that inlet spike movement and bypass door operations were almost as effective as elevons and rudders in influencing the aircraft's flight path at high speed. In addition, propulsion system and flight control integration was tested by NASA in an effort to improve future mixed compression inlet design.

Honeywell and Lockheed funded the Central Airborne Performance Analyser (CAPA). This was installed and tested by NASA and proved so successful that it was later fitted to the operational

Fitz Fulton and Ray Young were flying NASA's YF-12A for this formation flight with a T-38 chaseplane. Note the camera and experiment pods beneath the Blackbird. (Paul F. Crickmore Collection)

SR-71 fleet. This integrated automatic support system isolated faults and recorded the performance of 170 subsystems (relating primarily to the inlet controls), on 0.5-in (12.7-mm) magnetic tape. Pre- and post-flight analysis of this onboard monitoring and diagnostic system proved very cost effective and reduced maintenance man-hours significantly.

After its 88th NASA flight on 28 September 1978, the YF-12C was retired from the programme and placed in storage at Palmdale. YF-12A, 60-6935 continued operating until the programme ceased after its 145th NASA flight, which was flown by Fitz Fulton and Vic Horton on 31 October 1979. A week later, Col Jim Sullivan and Col R. Uppstrom ferried the aircraft to the Air Force museum at Dayton, Ohio, where it is displayed as the sole surviving example of the YF-12.

The most ambitious experiment to date got underway on 31 October 1997 and involved hauling the largest external load since Project Tagboard (the M-21/D-21 drone evaluations of 1964–66). The first flight, lasting one hour 50 minutes, marked the beginning of the Linear Aerospike SR-71 Experiment (LASRE), during which time aircraft 64-17980, NASA 844, reached a maximum speed of Mach 1.2 and altitude of 33,000 ft (10058 m). On 4 March 1998 the first of three cold-flow flights was made, during which gaseous helium and liquid nitrogen were cycled through the Boeing-Rocketdyne J2-S linear aerospike engine. However, numerous cryogenic leaks were discovered and despite the engine being 'hot fired' on the ground, on two occasions, for a total of three seconds, it was deemed to be too dangerous to fire-up the engine with its liquid hydrogen fuel while aloft. Investigation into the leaks determined that these would be too difficult and expensive to rectify, therefore the programme was cancelled in November 1998. Since participating in the Edwards AFB open house weekend of 9/10 October 1999, the NASA SR-71s have therefore been placed in 'flyable storage' while awaiting requests and funding for future 'access to space' projects.

NASA 844 is seen dumping water after the first inflight cold-flow test of the linear aerospike engine. (NASA Dryden Flight Research Center)

Appendix 2. Disposition

A-12

AF serial 60-6924, Lockheed Article Number 121
Prototype, now on display at Palmdale Air Museum, Nevada

60-6925, 122
Displayed onboard USS *Intrepid*. New York

60-6926, 123
Crashed 24 May 1963, pilot Ken Collins survived

60-6927, 124
Displayed at California Museum of Science, Los Angeles

60-6928, 125
Crashed 5 January 1967, pilot Walter Ray killed

60-6929, 126
Crashed 28 December 1967, pilot Mel Vojvodich survived

60-6930, 127
Displayed at Space and Rocket Museum, Huntsville, Alabama

60-6931, 128
Displayed at Minnesota ANG Museum, St Paul, Minneapolis

60-6932, 129
Crashed 5 June 1968, pilot Jack Weeks killed

60-6933, 130
Displayed at the Aerospace Museum, San Diego, California

60-6937, 131
Displayed at Birmingham Air Museum, Alabama

60-6938, 132
Displayed onboard USS *Alabama*, Mobile, Alabama

60-6939, 133
Crashed 9 July 1964, pilot Bill Park survived

60-6940, 134
Converted to M-21 to carry D-21 drone. Displayed at Museum of Flight, Seattle, Washington

60-6941, 135
Converted to M-21 to carry D-21 drone. Crashed 30 July 1966, pilot Bill Park survived, Launch Control Officer Ray Torrick killed

YF-12A

60-6934, 1001
Converted into SR-71 trainer, referred to as SR-71C, and re-serialled 64-1781, displayed at Hill AFB, Utah

60-6935, 1002
Displayed at the Air Force Museum, Wright Patterson AFB, Dayton, Ohio

60-6936, 1003
Crashed 24 July 1971, pilot and Fire Control Officer, Jack Layton and Bill Curtis both survived

SR-71

64-17950, 2001
Written-off on 10 January 1967, pilot Art Peterson survived

64-17951, 2002
Used by NASA as YF-12C 60-6937. Displayed at Pima Museum, Tucson, Arizona

64-17952, 2003
Crashed 25 January 1966, pilot Bill Weaver survived, RSO Jim Zwayer killed

64-17953, 2004
Crashed 18 December 1969, Pilot and RSO, Joe Rogers and Gary Heidelbaugh both survived

64-17954, 2005
Written-off 11 April 1969, pilot and RSO Bill
Skliar and Noel Warner both survived
64-17955, 2006
Displayed at the Air Force Flight Test Center
Museum, Edwards AFB, California
64-17956, 2007
SR-71B, with NASA in 2002, at Edwards AFB,
likely to be displayed at Kennedy Space Center,
Florida
64-17957, 2008
SR-71B, crashed 11 January 1968, instructor pilot
and 'student', Robert Sowers and Dave Fruehauf
both survived
64-17958, 2009
Displayed at Warner-Robbins AFB Museum,
Georgia
64-17959, 2010
Displayed at Eglin AFB, Florida
64-17960, 2011
Displayed at Castle AFB Museum, California
64-17961, 2012
Displayed at the Kansas Cosmosphere & Space
Center, Hutchinson, Kansas
64-17962, 2013
Displayed at the Imperial War Museum,
Duxford, England
64-17963, 2014
Displayed at Beale AFB, California
64-17964, 2015
Displayed at the Strategic Air Command
Museum, Omaha, Nebraska
64-17965, 2016
Crashed 25 October 1967, both pilot and RSO,
Roy St Martin and John Carnochan survived
64-17966, 2017
Crashed 13 April 1967, both pilot and RSO, Earle
Boone and 'Butch' Sheffield survived
64-17967, 2018
Displayed at Barkesdale AFB Museum,
Louisiana
64-17968, 2019
Displayed at Richmond Air Museum, Virginia
64-17969, 2020
Crashed 10 May 1970, both pilot and RSO, Willie
Lawson and Gil Martinez survived
64-17970, 2021
Crashed 17 June 1970, both pilot and RSO,
Buddy Brown and Mort Jarvis survived
64-17971, 2022
Displayed at Edwards AFB, California

64-17972, 2023
Displayed at the Smithsonian Air and Space
Museum, Washington, DC
64-17973, 2024
Displayed at the Blackbird Airpark, Palmdale,
California
64-17974, 2025
Crashed 21 April 1989, both pilot and RSO, Dan
House and Blair Bozek survived
64-17975, 2026
Displayed at March AFB Museum, California
64-17976, 2027
Displayed at the Air Force Museum, Wright-
Patterson AFB, Dayton, Ohio
64-17977, 2028
Written-off 10 October 1968, both pilot and RSO,
'Abe' Kardong and Jim Kogler survived
64-17978, 2029
Written-off 20 July 1972, both pilot and RSO,
Denney Bush and Jimmy Fagg survived
64-17979, 2030
Displayed at the History and Traditions
Museum, Lackland AFB, Texas
64-17980, 2031, NASA 844
To be displayed at NASA Dryden Test Center,
Edwards AFB, California
64-17981, 2000
So-called SR-71C, trainer replacement, displayed
at Hill AFB Museum, Utah

'962 first flew on 29 April 1966. In all it flew
2835.9 hours before being retired. It was the last
SR-71 to leave Det 1 at Kadena, and is the only SR-71
to be retired outside the US. It can be seen on display
at the Imperial War Museum, Duxford,
Cambridgeshire, UK. (Paul F. Crickmore)

Appendix 3. Records

The records listed below were verified at the time by the Federation Aeronautique Internationale (FAI), but it should be remembered that impressive as these figures are, they are not demonstrations of the aircraft's absolute capabilities. For example, on 20 November 1965, an A-12 attained speeds in excess of Mach 3.2 and a sustained altitude capability above 90,000 ft (27432 m). During the first operational deployment of a CIA A-12, from Area 51 to Kadena Air Base on the island of Okinawa, pilot Mele Vojvodich covered the distance in Article Number 131, in just six hours six minutes; had it not been for security considerations, this could easily have been recognised as a new transpacific speed record. With the passage of time, several earlier SR-71 records were broken by highly modified aircraft derived from the Mikoyan-Gurevich MiG-25 'Foxbat'. Given the spurious designation Ye-266, three aircraft were initially involved, correctly designated Ye-155R-1, R-3 and P-1. Later, a Ye-266M testbed, based on the MiG-25M interceptor, added further records, but the inability of the USSR to produce an operational aircraft that represented a serious threat to the SR-71 remains telling.

YF-12A Records

It is probably no coincidence that the date chosen to demonstrate some of the YF-12's awesome capabilities was 1 May 1965 – exactly five years to the day that Francis Gary Powers was shot-down by a Soviet SA-2 SAM whilst conducting an overflight in his U-2.

Record: Absolute Altitude – 80,257.86 ft (24390 m)
Crew: Pilot Col Robert L. 'Fox' Stephens, Fire Control Officer (FCO) Lt Col Daniel Andre
Aircraft: YF-12A, 60-6936

Record: Absolute Speed Over a Straight Course – 2,070.101 mph (3331.41 km/h)
Crew: Pilot Col Robert L. 'Fox' Stephens, FCO Lt Col Daniel Andre
Aircraft: YF-12A, 60-6936

Record: Absolute Speed Over a 500-km Closed Course – 1,688.889 mph (2717.929 km/h)
Crew: Lt Col Walter F. Daniel, FCO Maj. James P. Cooney
Aircraft: YF-12A, 60-6936

Record: Absolute Speed Over a 1000-km Closed Course – 1,643.041 mph (2644.146 km)
Crew: Pilot Lt Col Walter F. Daniels, FCO Maj. Noel T. Warner
Aircraft: YF-12A, 60-6936

SR-71 Records

The first major attention-grabbing SR-71 headlines were, undoubtedly, the transatlantic speed records, of which both still stood unbroken, over twenty-seven years later in 2002.

Record: 1 September 1974; Speed Over a Recognised Course – New York to London
Crew: Pilot Maj. James V. Sullivan, RSO Maj. Noel F. Widdifield
Distance: 3,490 miles (5617 km); time 1 hour

A pair of SR-71As, '958 and '962 (seen here) was used for the 1976 record attempts. Both had large white crosses painted on their undersides for calibration purposes. (Lockheed)

54 minutes 56.4 seconds
Aircraft: SR-71A, 64-17972

Record: 13 September 1974; Speed Over a Recognised Course – London to Los Angeles
Crew: Pilot Capt. Harold B. Adams, RSO Capt. William C. Machorek
Distance: 5,645 miles (9084 km); time 3 hours 47 minutes 35.8 seconds
Aircraft: SR-71A, 64-17972

Next came celebrations commemorating the United States bicentennial year:

Record: 27/28 July 1976; Altitude in Horizontal Flight – 85,068.997 ft (25929.031 m)
Crew: Pilot Capt. Robert C. Helt, RSO Maj. Larry A. Elliott
Aircraft: SR-71A, ???

Record: 27/28 July 1976; Speed Over a Straight Course (15-/25-km) – 2,193.167 mph (3529.56 km/h)
Crew: Pilot Capt. Eldon W. Joersz, RSO Maj. George T. Morgan
Aircraft: SR-71A, ???

Record: 27/28 July 1976; Speed Over a Closed Course (1,000-km) – 2,092.294 mph (3367.221 km/h)

Crew: Pilot Maj. Adolphus H. Bledsoe, RSO Maj. John T. Fuller
Aircraft: SR-71A, ???

Finally, despite all that some Strategic Air Command officials could do to prevent more headline grabbing after the programme was prematurely closed-down, more records were set in 1990.

Record: 6 March 1990; Speed Over a Recognised Course – Los Angeles to East Coast
Crew: Pilot Lt Col Ed Yeilding, RSO Lt Col Joseph T. Vida

Coast-to-Coast: 2,086 miles (4966 km); time 1 hour 7 minutes 53.69 seconds, average speed 2,144.83 mph (2451.67 km/h)

Los Angeles to Washington, DC: 1,998 miles (3215 km); time 1 hour 4 minutes 19.89 seconds, average speed 2,144.83 mph (3451.67 km/h)

St Louis to Cincinnati: 311.44 miles (501.20 km); time 8 minutes 31.97 seconds, average speed 2,176.08 mph (3501.97 km/h)

Kansas City to Washington, DC: 942.08 miles (1516.08 km); time 25 minutes 58.53 seconds, average speed 2,176.08 mph (3501.97 km/h)

Aircraft: SR-71A, 64-17972

Appendix 4. Model Kits and Further Reading

For further reading we would recommend the following:-

Lockheed SR-71 The Secret Missions Exposed, by Paul F. Crickmore and published by Osprey. ISBN 1-84176-098-6

Lockheed's Skunk Works, by Jay Miller and published by Midland Publishing Ltd. ISBN 1-85780-037-0

Available plastic model kits have included:

Kit	Scale/size
Academy, injection moulded	1:72
Hasegawa, injection moulded	1:72
Hobbycraft, injection moulded	1:288
Italeri, injection moulded	1:72
Reheat	120 mm long
Revell, injection moulded	Unknown
Testors, injection moulded	1:48
True Details, injection moulded cockpit detail set	1:48

Appendix 5. Glossary

AAA	Anti-Aircraft Artillery	ANS	Astro-inertial Navigation System
ADP	Advanced Development Projects	ARCP	Air Refuelling Control Point
ADS	Accessory Drive System	ARS	Air Refuelling Squadron
AFCS	Automatic Flight Control System	ASARS	Advanced Synthetic Aperture Radar System
AFSC	Air Force Systems Command	BDA	Bomb Damage Assessment
AICS	Air Inlet Control System	BUFF	Big Ugly Fat F***er (B-52)

CAP	Combat Air Patrol
cg	Centre of Gravity
CIA	Central Intelligence Agency
CINC	Commander In Chief
CIT	Compressor Inlet Temperature
CIS	Chemical Ignition System
COMINT	Communications Intelligence
CP	Control Point
DAFICS	Digital Automatic Flight Inlet Control System
DEF	Defensive Electronic System
Det	Detachment
DIA	Defense Intelligence Agency
Dipsy doodle	A manoeuvre used to aid acceleration to intermediate Mach numbers when the aircraft is heavy with fuel
DMZ	Demilitarised Zone
DoD	Department of Defense
DP	Destination Point
ECM	Electronic Countermeasures
Elint	Electronic Intelligence
EOB	Electronic Order of Battle
FAA	Federal Aviation Administration
FCF	Functional Check Flight
FCO	Fire Control Officer
GCI	Ground Controlled Intercept
Humint	Human Intelligence
IGV	Inlet Guide Vanes
INS	Inertial Navigation System
JCS	Joint Chiefs of Staff
KEAS	Knots Equivalent Airspeed
MPC	Mobile Processing Centre
NASA	National Aeronautics and Space Administration
NSA	National Security Agency
OBC	Optical Bar Camera
OSI	Office of Scientific Intelligence
PACAF	Pacific Air Force
PARPro	Peacetime Aerial Reconnaissance Program
PEM	Program Element Manager
PRF	Pulse Repetition Frequency
PRI	Pulse Repetition Interval
PSD	Physiological Support Division
Radint	Radar Intelligence
RTS	Reconnaissance Technical Squadron
RAM	Radar Absorbing Material
RCS	Radar Cross Section

RHAWR	Radar Homing and Warning Receiver
RSO	Reconnaissance Systems Officer
	Research Systems Operator (NASA operations only)
SAC	Strategic Air Command
SAM	Surface-to-Air Missile
SAS	Stability Augmentation System
Sigint	Signals Intelligence
SIOP	Single Integrated Operational Plan
SLAR	Side-Looking Airborne Radar
SPO	Systems Project Officer
SRC	Strategic Reconnaissance Center
SRS	Strategic Reconnaissance Squadron
SRW	Strategic Reconnaissance Wing
TDY	Temporary Duty
TEB	Tri-ethyl borane
TEOC	Technical Objective Camera
UCD	Urine Collection Device
Unstart	The condition where the normal shock wave entering the engine inlet is 'belched' forwards, causing a loss of thrust from the 'unstarted' engine

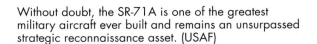

Without doubt, the SR-71A is one of the greatest military aircraft ever built and remains an unsurpassed strategic reconnaissance asset. (USAF)